THE
METRONOME
EFFECT

D0596129

THE METRONOME EFFECT

THE JOURNEY TO PREDICTABLE PROFIT

SHANNON BYRNE SUSKO

Advantage®

Copyright © 2014 by Shannon Byrne Susko

All rights reserved. No part of this book may be used or reproduced in any manner whatsoever without prior written consent of the author, except as provided by the United States of America copyright law.

Published by Advantage, Charleston, South Carolina.
Member of Advantage Media Group.

ADVANTAGE is a registered trademark and the Advantage colophon is a trademark of Advantage Media Group, Inc.

Printed in the United States of America.

ISBN: 978-159932-461-6
LCCN: 2014943065

Cover design by George Stevens.
Interior layout by Megan Elger.

This publication is designed to provide accurate and authoritative information in regard to the subject matter covered. It is sold with the understanding that the publisher is not engaged in rendering legal, accounting, or other professional services. If legal advice or other expert assistance is required, the services of a competent professional person should be sought.

Advantage Media Group is proud to be a part of the Tree Neutral® program. Tree Neutral offsets the number of trees consumed in the production and printing of this book by taking proactive steps such as planting trees in direct proportion to the number of trees used to print books. To learn more about Tree Neutral, please visit **www.treeneutral.com**. To learn more about Advantage's commitment to being a responsible steward of the environment, please visit **www.advantagefamily.com/green**

Advantage Media Group is a publisher of business, self-improvement, and professional development books and online learning. We help entrepreneurs, business leaders, and professionals share their Stories, Passion, and Knowledge to help others Learn & Grow. Do you have a manuscript or book idea that you would like us to consider for publishing? Please visit **advantagefamily.com** or call **1.866.775.1696**.

To my husband, Sko, and my children—
Cain, Matthew and Embyr-Lee—with Love.

Thanks for supporting me through all of these journeys.

acknowledgements

I would like to express my sincere gratitude to the many people who saw me through this book.

I would like to thank the Advantage Media team: especially Christa Bourg, Brooke White, George Stevens, Patti Boysen and Megan Elger for enabling me to publish this book.

Thanks to Verne Harnish for supporting me through my journey with Mastering the Rockefeller Habits and challenging me to find my metronome.

Thanks to ACETECH—first and foremost my CEO roundtable of 10+ years for the unending encouragement and support. The inaugural ACETECH Growth Strategy Program attendees for their interest, questions, and commitment to the program, and Kathy Troupe, Simon Cloutier, Liz Bowell, Paulin Laberge and Holly MacDonald for their excellent execution, enthusiasm and belief in the metronome effect.

I would like to thank the Paradata team of the time for their never-ending belief, their support to follow the untraditional and their commitment to the process.

I must also thank my co-founding partner of Subserveo, Mike Hagerman, for his enthusiastic encouragement and unwavering belief in this process. With this—a big thank you to the Subserveo team for continuing to challenge and evolve the metronome effect methodology.

Even though my father passed away in November 2006, he was an extraordinary example of a life long entrepreneur. I am so thankful for his entrepreneurial spirit, passion and guidance he provided through building his own companies. And I would be remiss not to express my deepest gratitude to my mother, the backbone of the Byrne family, for her consistent unwavering support for all my endeavours.

Above all I want to thank my husband, Sko and my three children, Cain, Matthew and Ember-Lee, who supported and encouraged me in spite of the time it took me away from them.

Last but not least: I beg forgiveness of all those who have been with me over the course of these years and whose names I have failed to mention.

"WE ARE WHAT WE REPEATEDLY DO.
EXCELLENCE, THEN, IS NOT AN ACT,
BUT A HABIT."

ARISTOTLE

FOREWORD BY VERNE HARNISH

Shannon is the real deal. While some people can "teach" and others can "do", Shannon can do both, scaling up and exiting several fast growth businesses and now helping other CEOs do the same. And along the way create companies that generate predictable profits in an unpredictable world.

I first met Shannon Byrne Susko at Canada's Top 40 Under 40™ Leadership Forum in April of 2001. I was hosting and moderating this three-day forum. Shannon, one of the forty leaders chosen from across Canada to participate, first approached me during a break. She wanted to know what a "daily huddle" was. Then, at the next break she was back asking about "Good News"—and then, at the next break, she wanted to learn more about our "one page plan." Shannon was thirsty for information on the best way to scale up her business. She knew she was at a point where change was required in order to grow further. For the rest of the forum, Shannon tried to drain as much information from me, and the other speakers, as possible (leaders are learners!).

About a month later, I received an email from Shannon with questions about the next steps, and then, the next month, another email. This went on for about a year. Shannon was working with her team to implement what is now called the Rockefeller Habits.

About two and a half years later I was moderator of the Business Development Bank of Canada's Young Entrepreneurs Forum. Shannon was the kickoff speaker. Her topic, unbeknownst to me, was how she had led her team through a full and successful implementation of the Rockefeller Habits over the last eight quarters. It blew me away.

Shannon is a student of strategy and execution. She has implemented the Rockefeller Habits methodology through four different companies: small-private, large-private, start-up and, finally, a large-public company. Shannon understands how to use the Rockefeller Habits to raise capital as well as manage two successful exits. As a young entrepreneur—and, still, 20 years later—she remains a ferocious reader and implementer of the practical strategic tools of the business thought leaders of our time.

Today, we're excited that Shannon is working with us as a Gazelles Certified coach who continues to fulfill her core purpose of helping others grow. This book is a testament to—and "how to" of—her philosophy. *The Metronome Effect* is drawn from Shannon's experience as CEO and is a prescriptive account of how she and her team incorporated some of the best strategic and execution tools of our time from thought leaders such as Jim Collins, Michael Porter, Patrick Lencioni, Brad Smart, Geoffrey Moore, and myself.

So I invite you to read, reflect and utilize Shannon's practical learning and experience gained through implementing and working with the Rockefeller Habits for over thirteen years. I hope you enjoy and learn from Shannon's journey in setting your metronome to drive *Predictable Profit*.

VERNE HARNISH, Founder, Gazelles and EO

Author: *Scaling Up* (Fall 2014); *The Greatest Business Decisions of All Time; Mastering the Rockefeller Habits*

CONTENTS

INTRODUCTION

I was recently the keynote speaker at a luncheon hosted by a software company. After I was introduced, I stood up in front of this roomful of people and started clapping. I didn't say anything; I just clapped. Pretty soon, a few people in the audience started clapping along with me. Then more people joined in. If I sped up, the room sped up with me. If I slowed down, the room slowed down with me. It wasn't long before the entire room was clapping together in unison.

Then I stopped clapping, but it did not matter. Everyone kept going. I could have left the room and I'm certain they would have continued clapping together in a steady rhythm for quite a while. I looked out over the crowd, and when they finally quietened down a bit, I said, 'Just remember this moment.'

That is the metronome effect.

A metronome is a device that produces a metrical beat. I used one when I practiced piano as a child. I've also used a kind of metronome or steady rhythm to build up two highly successful software companies to the point where we could sell them. Rhythm is a way to set expectations within an organization so that your team knows what they need to do to succeed. It's also a way for the leader to be sure that the strategy, a healthy organization, the human system, and the execution plan is being thought about regularly and focused on to drive profit.

As I continued with my speech, I asked the crowd, 'As a leader in your organization, what beat do you want to set? Because, if you create a strong disciplined beat, your team will fall into it, just like you all did here today. That is the best way to ensure that your team is always thinking about the strategic plan, execution plan, the team, and cash plan in order to make the best effort every day to drive the organization towards your goals.'

◆ ❖ ◆

This book has been written by an experienced CEO for other CEOs and high-level leaders. It's for anyone really who wants to predict profit and grow a business every year. The goal behind this book is to show you how you can make sure your company, or team, has a firm rhythm in place that incorporates team cohesiveness, strategy, execution, and your human system. All of the above should be built on a strong foundation of culture that is driven by the leader. The Metronome Effect methodology incorporates all aspects of your organization into one disciplined rhythm that beats each year, each quarter, each month, each week, and each day. As a leader, you have to have the discipline to instill the rhythm in your team, incorporating strategic tools, your team cohesiveness tools, your human system tools, and your cash tools. That is how the team will come to expect that this is a part of what you do as an organization. This book will show you how to establish that essential rhythm so that you can grow your strategy and your profit year after year.

One of the reasons I wanted to share the information in this book is because it works. This is a practical approach that all leaders can implement. This worked in my own companies, in the companies that bought my companies, and in those organizations that I've worked with as a strategic advisor and coach. It's been fantastic to watch organizations transform through the Metronome Effect.

When we started our first company, I did not know what I had signed up for. I am an avid reader and knew that others had faced what we were facing as we built a new technology company. I started reading two to four business books per week, looking for practical solutions to our challenges. The authors of these books were the top thought leaders of our time in business. I found a lot of useful information in their work, but I also realized that each thought leader offered just a piece of the puzzle. As a team, we were using all these tools, but in a very ad hoc way. I wanted to find a practical way to tie them all together, so we created our own methodology that encapsulated the best strategic tools and execution tools we could find at the time into one methodology. That's what you'll find in this book. It's a methodology that pulls together the thinking and research of some of the best business minds of our time and structures it all into one rhythm that you can follow year after year, quarter after quarter, month after month, week after week, day after day, to grow your organization. I recently taught this methodology to a group of about eighty CEOs. I told them, 'The rhythm will set you free. It will allow you to grow your strategy, grow your company, and predict your profit. You will have more time to spend thinking about the big-picture aspects of your business, not about how to manage the day-to-day grind of your business. And isn't that what we're all looking for—a practical approach to grow our team, evolve our strategy, execute, and predict profit?'

I have been a CEO since 1997. I think of myself as a serial entrepreneur. I have a business degree, a computer science degree, and a master's degree in computer science. Just after I graduated with my master's degree, I was very fortunate to cofound a company called Paradata Systems, Inc. that built a global payment system. That was where we ended up, but the first four years of that company were chaotic. They were the Internet bubble years, a high-growth time for the technology industry. The four founders—myself included—were very inexperienced at growing a technology company, and to be quite frank, none of us really knew what we were doing.

We raised a lot of investment in those early years for two different products; one failed, and we sold the intellectual property of the second to another company to allow us to focus on our payment platform. By the time we found our stride in the payment industry, the three other cofounders had left the organization to pursue other interests. I was, literally, left holding the bag with a lot of investors, a lot of money invested, remnants of technology products, and an Internet payment system.

That's when we learned how to stay focused on the payment system, which was in very high demand, and planned to grow it worldwide, which we did. We grew from four people to approximately eighty people in a year. I was on the road travelling approximately 90 percent of the time. It was chaotic, at best. We had a very experienced leadership team, but I was still looking for the silver bullet that would provide clarity, alignment, and precise execution of the plan. I was still reading ferociously.

Around that time, I happened to meet Verne Harnish at a leadership conference and learned about what would become the Rockefeller Habits. (This was before he published his book *Mastering the Rockefeller Habits*. Verne has revised and updated *Mastering the Rockefeller Habits*—the new book is called *Scaling Up: How to Build a Meaningful Business...and Enjoy the Ride,* which is being released in fall of 2014.) I was drawn to Verne Harnish's work because he had come up with a way to pull an entire strategic business plan together on one piece of paper. It was practical. It was one page! I'm a very visual person, so I loved how you could look at it and get an overall view of a business. I also loved how you could easily share the plan with shareholders, team members, board members, customers, and partners. It took eight quarters for us to fully implement Verne Harnish's framework. In doing so, we took other tools we had been using from a number of different thought leaders, including Jim Collins, Patrick Lencioni, and Michael Porter, and worked those into our rhythm.

Through the use of these tools and Verne Harnish's concept of a one page plan, we were able to align our team, bring clarity to the plan, integrate a deep sense of accountability, and implement a rhythm that did not miss a beat. My team and I were able to bring to market a global payment system. By focusing on that new payment process platform, we built the organization to the point where we were able to sell in January 2006.

Two years later, I cofounded a second company called Subserveo, Inc., which provided post-trade compliance solutions to broker-dealers in North America. This time, we used the Metronome Effect methodology from the start. As we grew from two people to twenty people and beyond, we again set the metrical beat to grow our company and predict our profit. We attracted people from teams I'd worked with before, because they knew what to expect: a strong culture where they could grow and participate in developing the strategy, clear execution plans, and a solid human system to support the team. They had worked within this framework in the past and had been able to grow themselves and grow the company. We were very clear that we wanted to build the company's value quickly and exit in a very short amount of time. By using this methodology, we were able to do just that. Only three years and three months after founding the company, we sold it for a valuation that was well above the industry average.

The Metronome Effect methodology works. It's not a silver bullet but a journey of habituation that will drive the excellence you require to succeed. The Metronome Effect pushes you to continuously write down your strategy in a succinct way and then continuously improve upon it. You must get comfortable with 'good enough' and 'gutting it out', because if you don't, you won't be able to move forward and grow. I have a lot of clients who get stuck on the tools outlined in this book. They freeze up when challenged to write something down even if it's far from perfect, because they want it to be just right before they move ahead. But in this methodology, perfection doesn't matter. What does matter is the discipline of the leader to establish the rhythm within which you are always evolving, always improving. In order to do that, you have to have a starting place. Start by writing something down.

This framework was founded on Verne Harnish's One Page Plan (OPP) methodology and ties into Patrick Lencioni's *Five Dysfunctions of a Team*, Jim Collins's research, Michael Porter's research, and Brad Smart's *Topgrading*. Throughout the book, I'll share stories of how we implemented these tools at both my companies to illustrate the profound effect they can have. And when I use the word 'we' in this book, I'm referring to the team I worked with at those companies, that helped me develop this methodology over the years. Working through these tools together, which is what I suggest throughout much of the book, has the added benefit of unlocking the collaborative mind of your team members so you can use the shared wisdom of the team, rather than having to rely on just your own knowledge in order to grow.

Together with my team, I have been using and developing these tools and the Metronome Effect methodology for over fourteen years. In addition to both the companies I cofounded, this methodology has also been implemented at the companies that acquired those companies, not-for-profit organizations, and many other organizations I have worked with as a strategic advisor. I've brought this methodology to organizations in a wide variety of industries—from a company that builds cement blocks to one that delivers educational programs, to another in the airline aviation space, and more. These experiences have shown me that it doesn't matter what kind of company you are in. As long as you consciously set the beat of a metronome to grow your business and follow it consistently and with discipline, this methodology can work for you.

Jim Collins has proven in his work that the most successful growth companies have three basic things in common: (a) habits that equal discipline, (b) a culture of continuous learning, and (c) accountability mechanisms in place. This rhythm I keep talking about will help you make sure you have all these things working for you, and then, once the rhythm is established, you don't have to think about it anymore. It doesn't matter what your rhythm is as long as it's consistent across your organization. If it is consistent, the beat will continue just like that of a metronome. You count on your metronome to keep beating every day without you having to make it happen. That's the kind of rhythm I'm talking about. It's the Metronome Effect that becomes the heartbeat of an organization, and everybody learns to expect it to beat at a certain speed.

In order to create that rhythm in my companies, we set very specific daily, weekly, monthly, quarterly, and annual activities—not just meetings—all of which will be covered throughout this book. And once the metronome was set, I had the pleasure of watching my firms and my team members grow, knowing that the cadence would continue no matter what happened.

HOW TO USE THIS BOOK

At the end of this chapter, you'll find a drawing that looks like a house. This house represents the Metronome Effect methodology to show what key elements should be involved in growing your team, strategy, execution plan, and your human system. The synchronization of these elements will ensure your ability to predict your profit. The various parts of that 'house', from the leader at the foundation to the team on the top, make up the chapters in this book. We're going to build a rhythm for growth into your organization in the same way that one builds a house, step by step, piece by piece, from foundation to roof. Once the framework of this house is in place, we will never stop developing the elements or the building blocks of the house. These constant activities will keep the lights on and the 'electricity' flowing.

The tools and best practices of a number of thought leaders are integrated into this step-by-step methodology so that you don't have to search for the information you need. You won't have to do what I did in the beginning, which was to read four business books a week for nearly four years. I have gathered the best and most important tools in one place to cover all the crucial aspects of growing your strategy and profit. Finding time to grow your business while still finding your life balance is always difficult. Let this book be your shorthand guide to the best business tools and wisdom, and once you have your rhythm in place, once you have created the Metronome

Effect, I highly recommend that you return to it regularly. You can dip back into it at any time, in any chapter, to brush up on a specific area of your business. This book is meant to be a practical resource that you can use, no matter what you're focused on at a particular moment, rather than something you need to sit down and read cover to cover. That's why each chapter ends with Action Items, essential steps you *must* take in order to move forward. Reading through these Action Items on a regular basis is a great way to make sure you're staying on track in each of the areas covered in this book.

The Metronome Effect methodology can help you, whether you've just started a business or you've been in business for forty years. It works whether you're a tiny start-up or a global organization. Regardless of what kind of company they're in, all CEOs and top leaders have something that keeps them up at night. Whether that thing is cash to grow, the right people, confidence in their strategy, execution planning, a healthy organization, a human system, or something else, it's almost certainly covered in this book.

When I say that the rhythm will set you free, I mean that it will help you be confident that you're doing everything you need to do to grow your business and that you're doing these things on a regular basis so nothing is overlooked.

Sidebars throughout the book, which I call 'Setting the Beat', will remind you to build these steps right into your calendar so that you're working them on a regular basis. Once you do that, you can rely on that rhythm to drive growth in your business and confidently predict your profit.

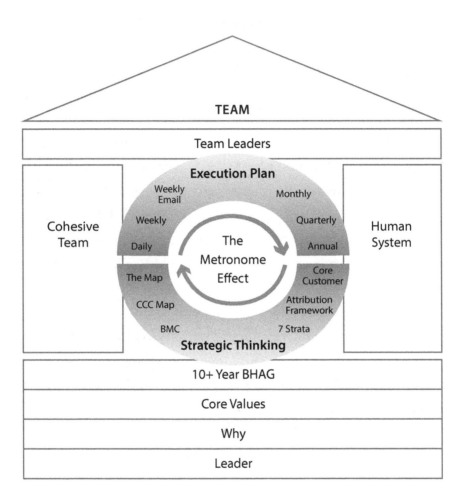

CHAPTER 1

THE LEADER

The first step in building a house is to lay the foundation. If you refer back to the house image at the end of the introduction, you'll see that the leader is at the bottom, serving as the foundation of any organization.

Being an effective leader requires a certain level of self-awareness. Leaders need to understand why they show up every day. They need to understand what they are good at and what they are not good at. Sharing this information with their team is critical. They also require a deep understanding of what makes their team members tick, what they are good at and not good at. Finally, leaders need to be able to paint a clear, memorable picture of where they want the company to be in ten or more years.

YOUR PERSONAL 'WHY'

As the leader of an organization, you need to understand your 'why'— not the company's 'why', but your personal one. This involves little more than asking yourself the question of what gets you up every day and motivates you to go to the office.

There is no wrong answer here. It could be something as simple as 'I'm passionate about our purpose'. It could be that you want to grow your company in order to sell it. Leaders have all sorts of reasons why they do what they do, but the most important thing is that you understand your motivation and that you help others to understand it, too.

When we started my first company, Paradata Systems, Inc., I knew I wanted to be part of an organization where I was really happy to come to work every day, but also where I was happy to leave when my day was over. For me, being happy meant being part of a team that shared my core values. In the past, with some of the jobs I've had, I'd get up in the morning not looking forward to going to work. But at Paradata, I wanted to be able to say, 'Wow, I can't believe they pay me to show up every day!' And that's what happened. I was really excited to show up every day and work with this great group of people.

In addition, I wanted to build a company that someone else would value. In other words, the plan was to build it up and then sell it off. Paradata was started in 1995, on the edge of the Internet bubble years, when lots of people were building companies and selling them for lots of money. We had taken on shareholders and we intended to give them a big return on their investment.

Those were my two personal 'whys': to create a great working environment that my team and myself would value, and to create a great organization that others would value so we could sell it and provide a return to shareholders.

Those 'whys' are pretty personal and not at all the 'why' of the company. When I'm working in my role as an advisor or coach with CEOs and other business leaders, I start by asking what their own 'why' is and they will answer with the company's 'why'. It's important to know that, too (and I'll talk more about it in Chapter 3), but that's not what we're talking about here. Many leaders have trouble understanding the difference. Understanding your personal why is about self-awareness, about understanding what drives you to work those hundred-hour weeks. It's about understanding why you get up every day and swing for the fence. Why did you take this risk?

I was coaching a client from a company that had been spun off from a larger organization that had been around for years. When I asked about the leader's 'why', he answered with the big 'why' of the company. It was a great company 'why', but it just didn't add up as a personal 'why'. The company was struggling, and he had a lot on the line. He would have to put in a lot of blood, sweat, and tears to turn this company around. Still, I couldn't pull out of him or his team why they wanted to go through that each and every day.

But I kept asking, and we finally got to the bottom of it. These people had worked their entire careers for others. They had done a really good job of helping other people build up their companies, and then they had watched as those people walked away with liquidity when the companies were sold. Now, they wanted the same thing for themselves. They had ownership stakes in a company for the first time, and they wanted to hit the ball out of the park so they could reap the rewards.

They were actually quite shy about saying it, but the real reason why they were willing to fight hard to make the company work was that they believed that if they succeeded, the business would produce a great life for them and enable them to provide well for their families. That's a compelling 'why'. They didn't need to tell everyone else what their motivation was if they didn't want to, but they had to at least understand it themselves.

At my second company, Subserveo, Inc., the cofounder and I had a personal 'why' that we didn't share with everyone. We were aiming for a three- to five-year exit from the company because we wanted to be able to stop growing technology companies for a while and stay home with our young kids. Our whole goal was to create enough of a financial foundation for ourselves so that we could spend time with our kids while they were still young and wanted us around. We knew the amount of risk in growing a company, but we also knew that if we followed and implemented the Metronome Effect methodology by Setting the Metronome from day one to grow our strategy and profit, we would substantially decrease this risk.

At just three years in, we got two offers to buy the company and we knew exactly what our selling barometer was. We knew it because we understood our 'whys', both personal and organizational. We did the math and looked at whether it satisfied the 'why' of all our stake-holders as well as ourselves. As it turned out, the math was favourable for all, so we ended up selling the company.

In contrast, I know a CEO whose goal is to build a big Canadian company. That's an awesome 'why', and because I know his 'why', I can understand his reaction to our sale of Subserveo. 'I would never sell my baby', he said. His 'baby' is his company, of course. He and I have very different 'whys', which leads to very different futures for our companies.

What I've found in working with so many different people on their personal 'why' is that the leader sometimes thinks her 'why' is obvious, only to find out that her team members think it's something else or have no idea. Then there are the leaders who have trouble answering the question of why, even for themselves. Still others know their 'whys' but don't want to admit to them. Maybe you show up to work every day because you've got a mortgage to pay. That's OK. You've still got to have that self-awareness. I don't really care why leaders do what they do, but I believe they have to have a passionate reason for showing up every day, even if it's a self-interested one.

Not everyone needs to know your 'why', but it's really important for team cohesiveness that your team members understand it. They need to know what the leader is all about. Those clients who were so shy about admitting they worked hard because they wanted to make a boatload of money felt relieved when they finally told me the truth. I said to them, 'You should talk to your team members about your "why". People can get behind a personal "why" as much as they can a company "why". And they might even have the same "why".'

SETTING THE BEAT

FOUR STEPS FOR FINDING YOUR PERSONAL 'WHY'

Answer the following questions and use the answer to create your personal core purpose statement on the next page:

1. Reflect on your journey through high school and university. Do you see any repeating themes?

2. Look back over your work experience and career. Do you see any repeating themes? Do you see any that overlap with your educational experience?

3. What are the three most important things in your life today?

4. When you wake up in the morning, are you excited to walk out of the door to go to your workplace? If so, why? If not, why not?

PERSONAL CORE PURPOSE

We all have a reason to get up every day and spend most of our time on something.

> Why do you get up every day to spend your time on this something?
>
> People's 'whys' can change, so make sure you ask yourself the question of why you're showing up for work every day and confirm or change your answer **at least once every quarter**. If you find yourself waking up in the morning and saying, 'Ugh, I don't want to go there anymore', that's your signal that it's time to find a new opportunity that supports your 'why'.

KNOWING YOUR STRENGTHS AND WEAKNESSES

In my journey as a leader, the more self-aware I became, the better off my team and company were, but self-awareness can be hard to come by for a leader. As a CEO, you don't get a lot of feedback from your team. You might get formal feedback from your board, if you have one, but if you don't have one, you may not get any feedback at all. So, I have always looked to my team to give me feedback, and to the work of thought leaders to help me gain insight.

In my early days as a leader, I spent time putting in place a method for giving feedback to my team on a regular basis and getting feedback from them in return. These weren't traditional reviews; they were sit-down-and-have-a-coffee-and-a-discussion reviews that followed a set framework. Both myself and my team members came to these meetings having thought about and filled out a one page review. The reviews my team members gave me helped me build my self-awareness. I didn't always want to hear what they had to say, but since they worked many hours with me, I had to take their views pretty seriously and make adjustments where necessary.

During the chaotic time when I was launching my first company, I found one book that really gave me a lot of perspective on this subject. It was Patrick Lencioni's *The Five Temptations of a CEO*. I have made it part of my continuing growth as a leader to read that book every year. It's short and easy to read, and I get something different out of it every time. As a person, you're growing and changing all the time, and your business is, too. Reading that book allows me to quickly assess what my biggest temptation is at any given moment and compare it to what it has been in the past.

For example, after four years at Paradata, I discovered that my biggest temptation was to choose popularity over accountability. I was just happy that people showed up for work every day. For whatever reason, I wanted to be liked by my team more than I wanted to hold them accountable. Somebody would get a project 80 percent of the way done, and at the end of the week, I would review it and say, 'Oh, isn't that great? Thank you very, very much.' Then I would spend the rest of my weekend finishing the remaining 20 percent.

One weekend, while I was finishing up yet another project, I wondered why this kept happening. I was working with an executive coach at the time, and he pointed out that while I was good at laying out what I expected, I was not so good at holding people accountable for meeting those expectations. Together we figured out a couple of reasons why that might be. One was that those were the bubble years and great people were hard to find. Another was that the company was made up of a lot of people I had gone to school with, so the relationships were personal and in one-on-one situations I would let people off the hook.

From this analysis came two key realizations. One was that I had to find a way to hold my team accountable, and the other was that I needed the discipline to regularly take a step back and look at my biggest temptation as a leader. One key and simple action I took as a result was to reread Lencioni's book once a year so I could gauge what my biggest temptation was at that point in time. This was put into my calendar right away as a recurring appointment, and it has become part of my annual rhythm, a way to hold myself accountable for growing myself as a leader. The other result is something that has become deeply engrained in the Metronome Effect methodology, which is peer accountability. This will be discussed in Chapter 7. It is one of the key reasons for my companies' success and is also critical to the most successful companies.

If you're a self-aware leader, you have to understand what you're good at and what you're not good at, and that may change over time. That's why you have to work on this on a regular basis and make it part of your rhythm. By reading the same book year after year, I have created a methodology for checking in with myself and confirming whether I'm still weak in a particular area or whether I've improved or am weak in another area. My self-analysis never stops.

I also make sure my team knows about my weaknesses. Sharing this takes some of the pressure off me, because there are others who can fill in and support me when I slip. It also shows my team that I hold myself accountable to them and that I trust them enough to be honest with them. A lack of self-awareness can really turn off your best team members, your A players, and so can refusing to admit your flaws and thinking you're the smartest person in the room. If I'm honest, I know my team members already see my weaknesses whether I own up to them or not. Besides that, your lack of self-awareness and your team members' lack of self-awareness can really slow the pace of growth.

SETTING THE BEAT

To begin setting a rhythm for yourself that ensures professional growth, read *The Five Temptations of a CEO* by Patrick Lencioni once a year. It will help you continually build your self-awareness as a leader.

KNOWING YOUR TEAM

There are two key things I've always done as a leader and continue to do to this day: I spend a lot of time learning about myself and a lot of time learning about my team. Your team is your number-one priority. When I was at Subserveo, in order to continue to get very clear about what I, as a leader, was good at and not so good at, I read the book *Strengths Finder 2.0* by Tom Rath. Just as I have with *The Five Temptations of a CEO*, I have used it every year since.

The book covers thirty-four common strengths and offers an online assessment that helps you figure out which ones are your strengths and which are your weaknesses. I not only did this myself, I got my whole executive team to read the book and take the online assessment. We created a map with the results and posted it on the wall. It mapped out everybody's strengths. By sharing this information, we could visualize how our strengths fitted together and how we balanced each other's weaknesses. It was fascinating. It improved our communication tenfold within a twenty-four-hour period, just from being able to see clearly who was good at what. I could also begin to see where we might have a hole in our team, or if somebody was in a role that really didn't fit his strengths.

One of the reasons why it's so important for the leader to be self-aware is so she can bring that self-awareness to the team. In my view, the leader has to own the task of ensuring that people, who are the number-one asset of any organization (that's right out of Jim Collins's work), are in the right places and doing the right things.

In addition to knowing the strengths and weaknesses of each of your team members, you want to know their core values. How many times have you seen a new CEO come in to an organization and terminate most or all of the existing executives and bring in an entirely new executive team? CEOs do this because the old executive team do not share their same core values. We'll talk more about this in Chapter 3, but the key things to understand here are that you want to hire team members who share your core values, and that your core values stem from who you are as a leader. Building an awareness of yourself and your team members will help you know if you have the right fit.

SETTING THE BEAT

Using the Strengths Finder assessment and mapping the strengths of all your team members is a great exercise to use on a regular basis and when someone new joins your team. We kept our strengths map of our whole team up on the wall, and it grew over time. If you haven't assessed your own strengths in the past three years, I encourage you to do it now. Strengths can shift over time, and keeping up with those changes will help you grow as a leader. My best recommendation is to look at this map often. Keep it on the wall where all can view it and regularly review your strengths—**at minimum on an annual basis.**

PAINTING THE PICTURE

The leader is going to be the one who paints the picture of what the future looks like for your business. In working with so many CEOs, I've often been surprised by how few have a long-term picture of what they want the company's future to be. I believe that having this view is vital for all leaders who want to grow their organization's strategy and profit.

A lot of people will say, 'Oh yeah, I've got the picture in my head.' But that's not enough. Not only do you have to have a view of the future, you also need to be able to articulate it—simply and clearly. It's very hard for your team members to make good decisions if they don't have a clear view of where they're going. As the leader, you can't make all the decisions yourself, so you must be able to communicate that picture in a succinct, easy-to-understand way.

Don't be surprised if your picture changes over time, either. When I think back to the picture we painted at Subserveo, I realize just how much it evolved as we got more and more into the business.

SETTING THE BEAT

PAINTING YOUR PICTURE

Download the Painting Your Picture tool at www.metronome-effect. com. This tool has been adapted from Cameron Herold's book *Double Double*:

Describe what your company looks like 10 years from now as you walk around your offices.

What do you see?	What is marketing like? Are you marketing goods/services globally now? Are you launching new online and TV ads?
What do you hear?	How is the company running day to day? Are you focused on strategy, team building, customer relationships?
What are clients saying?	What do the company financials reveal?
What does the media write?	How are you funded?
What kinds of comments are your team members making at the water cooler?	How are your core values being realized among your employees?
What is the buzz in your community?	

Acknowledgement: Adapted from Cameron Herold's *Double Double*

ENSURING YOUR PERSONAL GROWTH

Leaders who are self-aware will set a rhythm to ensure their own personal growth. This is the foundation of the Metronome Effect methodology. For the past fourteen years or more, I have built into my annual calendar at least two classroom or conference-type professional development opportunities. I also read a minimum of twelve business books a year. Why am I still doing these things? Because, as a leader, I believe you've always got to be searching for a better way to do things. That's how you hold yourself accountable to your team. That's why people want to be on your team. As Jim Collins notes, the most successful companies are forever learning and improving. The great news about the Metronome Effect methodology is it helps you make sure you're doing just that: setting a beat to grow yourself.

ACTION ITEMS

1. Know your personal 'why'—what gets you up every morning to go to work? Write this down and review it regularly to make sure it's still compelling.

2. Read Patrick Lencioni's *The Five Temptations of a CEO*. Write down your biggest temptation and share it with team members.

3. Read *Strengths Finder 2.0* by Tom Rath and use the online assessment tool to determine your biggest strengths and weaknesses. Have your team members do this, too, and create a map showing how everyone's strengths and weaknesses fit together.

4. Download Cameron's Herold's adapted tool from www.metronome-effect.com. This tool will create a picture of what you want the future of your organization to look like. Share that picture with your team members.

5. Look for opportunities for personal growth and put them in your calendar today. These could mean attending classes or conferences or reading business books—anything that helps you build self-awareness and takes your leadership skills to the next level.

CHAPTER 2

FOUNDATION FOR PREDICTABLE PROFIT—
TEAM, ENVIRONMENT, AND CASH

In order to grow, you have to be able to attract a great team of people, you have to have cash, or access to cash, to fuel your growth, and you have to know whom you are playing or interacting with in your business and industry. I like to think of these three things as your foundation for growth. Each of these elements will come back into play later on, as we go through the Metronome Effect methodology, but touching on them early will set up an awareness of where you are in your business today. And that awareness will help you see how you can leverage these elements and drive your company towards predictable profit.

TEAM

Practically all the top CEOs in the world would say that if they didn't have the right people—which leads to the right culture for their team's success—they wouldn't have seen quarter-over-quarter, year-over-year growth. That's been proven in Jim Collins's book *Good to Great*. So we tackle people first, because without great people in the right positions, doing the right things, it's very hard to grow. When you are considering your people, the first question to ask yourself (based on ideas of the thought leaders Jim Collins and Verne Harnish) is whether you would enthusiastically rehire everyone on your team.

As a leader, you must ask yourself that question and honestly answer it, as well as get your team leaders to ask it about their own team members, on a regular basis (at least every ninety days). If the answer is no, this becomes a key area for examination and immediate action.

To fully answer the question, you really need to break it down and find the answers to three more questions. The first one, which Jim Collins puts forth in *Good to Great*, is 'What are my key seats?' To put it another way, Verne Harnish developed this question and drove leaders to ask, 'What are the key functional positions within my organization?' Next, Jim Collins insists you ask, 'Do I have the right people in those seats?' And finally, 'Is everyone in those seats doing the right things?'

Verne Harnish created a tool—a functional review chart called the 'Function Accountability Chart (FACe)', which I recommend you review with your leadership team at least quarterly. It will prompt you and your team to write down who is playing which functional role and how that team member is measured. This will give you and your team clarity on the different roles in your business and who is accountable for results in each functional area.

The idea behind this chart is to give you a really clear visual so you can quickly see your functional positions and where there are gaps or overlaps. Some functional roles might have two or more names beside them, which basically means no one is truly accountable for that role. Others might be empty, with no names attached. Or you might find that you have one name in four positions, which means someone is being stretched too thin. There are often a lot of aha! moments when you first fill out this chart, so take your time.

Before we found this tool, my company, Paradata, had been churning through people for about five years. It was a chaotic time of rapid growth and even though we had great people on our team, we didn't have everyone in the right place. I mentioned, before, that when I was a young CEO, my temptation, to use Patrick Lencioni's wording, was "popularity over accountability." I was very poor at holding people accountable. The discipline of working with my team to come to an agreement about who was responsible for what helped to make it very clear. With such visibility, ownership of roles and how team members would be measured and accountable to the team were clear.

It's really hard to grow without taking a step back and looking at your people. And not just once, as you read this chapter, but regularly. Some companies might look at this tool once a year, but I highly recommend doing it every ninety days because things change often, especially in high-growth companies. This kind of review was a part of our quarterly meeting preparation and an agenda item on our quarterly standing agenda. Take the time now to fill out a functional chart for your team and ask yourself if you still have the right people in the right functional roles doing the right things within your organization.

SETTING THE BEAT

Every quarter, ask yourself whether you would enthusiastically rehire everyone on your team. Break that question down to ask yourself three key things:

1. What are the key seats or functions within my organization?

2. Do I have the right people in those seats?

3. Are the right people doing the right things?

Every quarter, confirm or update the information on Verne Harnish's chart, the Function Accountability Chart (FACe).

THE ENVIRONMENT

The next step is to create what I call The Map. I didn't get this tool from a thought leader or a book but, rather, developed it myself as it was a way to create a picture of the market we were playing in. This is really important for every business leader, and I wish I had done it when I began my first company. The idea behind The Map is to show all the different organizations that your company interacts with at some level, companies that you sell through, your channels, suppliers you work with, partners you're leveraging, associations you're a member of, and also your competitors, so that you have a map of your business landscape.

It's very simple to do. Just take a blank piece of paper and put your company's name in the middle of the page. Then, on the left-hand side, write down all the entities involved in getting your product to market. This could be your customers, or a particular customer segment, or a channel that you sell through, whether directly or indirectly. There might also be someone who refers business to your company because you have complementary products.

Next, on the right-hand side of the page, you're going to create a map of your supply chain. Write down any suppliers you use to get your product/service to market. You might have supply chains for many different products, but you'll see, as you write them down, who your key suppliers are. On this side of the page I also include any partners or industry associations that the company is a member of. And finally, because they're also in our market landscape and we bump into them, even though we might not have a direct relationship with them, I include my direct competitors. This gives you a view of who is interacting with your market environment and with the same suppliers, channels partners, and customers.

I highly recommend that, as the leader, you try drawing The Map first. Then, take an hour or two with your leadership team and go through the process of drawing it together. Don't show them The Map you created, but instead, draw a new one from scratch to ensure you get input from your whole team.

As you do this, you'll start to see which are the most powerful organizations in your market environment. Drawing The Map and seeing all the players in one place helped our team realize that we were actually missing some key relationships, and that one company had a dual relationship with our organization.

Because of that experience, drawing The Map was the very first thing we did when the idea for my second company was presented, even before we had a team, a plan, or even any cash to fund it. We needed to understand the industry, the industry flow, and where the organization we were talking about creating could fit into the marketplace, and we needed to know whom we were going to make happy, whom we were going to annoy, and whom we could leverage to scale the business quickly. It was like understanding the ecosystem of a lake and what could happen when something new is introduced into that system. Where I grew up in Canada, at my family's cottage, is a lake that once had trout and salmon but no bass. When I was about sixteen, someone introduced bass stock into it, which had a tremendous unanticipated impact. Now, thirty years later, I go back to my cottage at the lake in the summer and there are no longer any salmon, trout, turtles, or leeches. There are just bass. That's the kind of effect you want to predict, visualize, and address.

One of the things I suggest you do for your new company is to forget about drawing your company's box in the center. You might not even have a company yet. You might just be evaluating an opportunity as I did for my second company, Subserveo. I sat down with an expert in the industry and wrote down the names of everybody who played in the broker-dealer market. I wanted to know how you buy stock, how you sell stock, what happens after the transaction takes place, where the information flows, who touches the stock, and who gets paid. I was looking for the full 360-degree view. I wanted to know what the broker-dealer 'lake' looked like. I drew it all out first, and then I asked what would happen if we brought a new company, my 'bass fish', into this lake. This view was critical, and it was key to deciding whether we should bring that product/service and that company to the market.

That map lived on our war room wall. We would review and update it regularly, at least every ninety days. It was a great visual way for the leadership team to walk into our quarterly meetings, look at The Map on the wall, and confirm that our environment was still the same. Or, if it wasn't the same, we discussed and made changes to The Map. As the years go by, markets change, of course. Companies buy companies, suppliers merge, competitors merge, competitors die and go away, and customer segments go away because of new technology. We captured that entire evolution on our map and ensured we were in a position of strength.

I once ran a session, with about sixty CEOs, at which I took them through the exercise of drawing their own maps. When we were through, about 80 percent of them said that they had never created a view like that before and that it was one of the most valuable things they had done that year. During the process, one of those CEOs realized that one of his biggest channel partners was also one of his biggest suppliers. So, this particular company was on both sides of his map. He brought this up in the session, and I said, 'OK, so now that you see that, what are you going to do about it?' He said, 'I've got a group in my organization thinking of this company as a channel, and I have another group in my organization thinking it's a supplier. I have to get these two groups together, internally, to approach this organization in a more strategic way.'

A similar situation happened at Subserveo when we drew our map. We were able to identify some pretty key strategic partners in the early stages of building the company, including one that was both a channel and a supplier. Drawing our map made it clear how very important this relationship was. But we also realized that we didn't want to bring the business development arm together with the operational supplier of the organization until we had enough customer momentum to leverage more business. And that's what we did. We waited until we had built up a significant base of customers and then we went to the top executives of the other organization and said, 'Hey, we have a good mass of your customers now using our platform. A lot of your salespeople are referring business to us, informally, and we are already connected to your platform. Let's put something formal in place so that we can leverage more of the market together. You can add value to your existing customers by offering our services, and we can grow by offering our services to more customers.' It became a highly successful relationship, and we went on to leverage this model to the biggest suppliers in the marketplace. I don't think we would have seen the opportunity so clearly if we hadn't drawn The Map. And I do not believe we would have leveraged the 'power' in our approach unless the whole team had been able to see how we were positioned.

The Map is also useful when you're looking to gain a strategic partner or another customer segment. You might try to draw a new approach on The Map and realize you can't do it properly without conflict. Maybe it's going to cut out one of your referral partners, or some other conflict.

As you continue reading this book, you'll notice I refer back to The Map along the way. You can overlay a lot of things on The Map once you get all the connections in place. Take the time to draw The Map with all the constituents in your market and connect them with lines so you can see clearly who is related to whom. Once you have a handle on the lay of the land, you can look at it in relation to cash flow or with a competitive view. You can look at it in relation to your business model. This map can have many, many layers, and it really enables your business plan to become very visual.

SETTING THE BEAT

The Map is a high-level view of all parties your organization interacts with in your market place. Writing down every player that interacts with, or impacts, your business will help you visualize where your organization fits in the market. Confirm or update your map **every quarter** with your team.

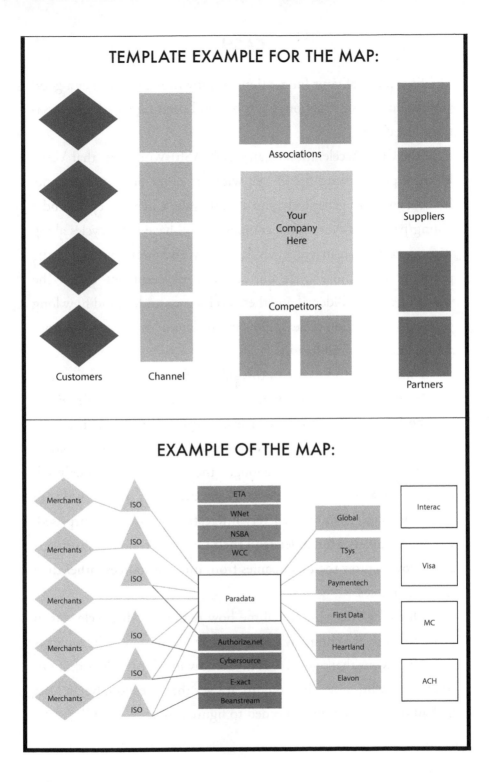

CASH

The final piece of your foundation for growth is cash. To get a good view of your cash situation, I recommend creating a cash conversation flow chart.

The Cash Acceleration Strategies (CASh) Worksheet that Verne Harnish puts forward fits in well with the other pieces we've done. It's broken down generically into a sales cycle, a delivery cycle, and a billing/payments cycle. Most companies will have these cycles along with a production/inventory cycle. In my companies we called the production/inventory cycle our software development cycle. The whole idea behind identifying these cycles is to understand how long your cash conversion cycle is. How many days does it take to go from a sales lead to cash in hand?

I was leading a session on this subject for a group of about sixty CEOs and, in the entire room, only two leaders were able to tell me the length of their cash conversion cycle. The companies represented in the room were anywhere from a couple of years old to forty years old. Interestingly enough, the CEOs could quickly tell me their payables, billing cycle, and sales cycle, but not the full cash conversion cycle. I found that very interesting but was not surprised. Company leaders who understand their cash conversion cycle understand how to grow their companies from internal sources rather than external sources.

One CEO was able to tell me how many days his cycle was in 2012 and how the company had already reduced its cycle by ten days this year. 'Wow, that's great,' I said. 'So how much cash does that put back in your business?' He couldn't answer that question, but at least he had the information he needed to figure it out.

What we're trying to do with this view of the business is to recognize that by focusing on the internal cycles of your business, you will identify internal cash you can use for growth. As Verne Harnish points out in his Cash Optimization Worksheet, there's always cash to be found, and normally, it's through eliminating mistakes in these cycles, or shortening the cycle by some operational efficiency or improvement, or by improving your business model.

We got some valuable insight into how we could find more cash for growth in my second business, Subserveo, when we came across *Behind the Cloud*, a book about Salesforce.com by founder and CEO, Mark Benioff. At one point, Salesforce.com was having trouble with its cash flow, and one of the board members said, 'Hey, we're a software-as-a-service business. We're a subscription-based business, and our users pay month to month. Why don't we ask our existing customers to pay for an annual subscription up front instead?'

Salesforce.com did just that. Being paid up front really shortened its cash conversion cycle, which put it in a very strong cash position. Subserveo was an SaaS business as well, so we were very grateful for this lesson. We immediately added to our contract two very simple things: the price for a month-to-month service option—and we actually increased the amount—and an annual option. We made that the cheaper option. We put two boxes next to these prices, asking people to check one, and we included space for a credit card number.

My cofounding partner at the time believed no one would pay up front for the whole thing and no one would pay by credit card. But it only took about thirty seconds to add this to the contract, so we did it anyway to see what would happen. We sent out the new contract and, sure enough, the first client who received it checked the annual payment box and gave us his credit card information. That instantly changed our cash flow situation. It gave us cash up front, which helped us grow faster.

CASH CONVERSION FLOW CHART

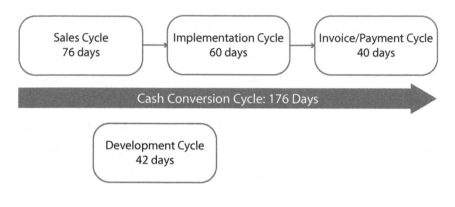

CASH CONVERSION FLOW CHART:
SALES CYCLE—76 DAYS

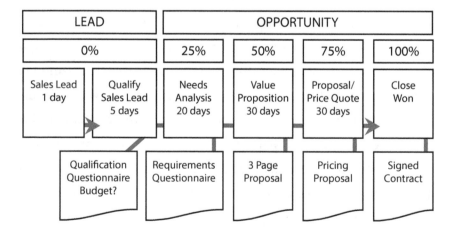

We took Verne Harnish's worksheet one step further, and I recommend you do so as well. Not only did we identify the cycles and come up with ways to shorten them, but we drew a high-level flow chart for our cash conversion cycle, and then, for each cycle, drew a more detailed flow chart. This allows you and your team a more detailed view of these important cycles/processes in your business. This, again, was kept on our war room wall and updated on a regular basis. The above diagram gives you an idea of what it could look like for your organization.

Each cycle in our organization was 'owned' by a team leader, who was responsible for ensuring the cycle was as short as possible. We kept track of our progress month over month and quarter over quarter through colouring key stages in the cycle red, yellow, or green, representing levels of efficiency. In the areas where we were doing well, we coloured the boxes green. Where we thought we could improve, we coloured them yellow. And the ones that were red needed to change. We worked on the cycle quarter after quarter, reviewing it, as a group, every ninety days.

I find that new companies are more religious about keeping up this kind of regular focus on their cash conversion cycle flow chart than older companies are. While working with a group of CEOs, I asked whose companies were profitable, and lots of people raised their hands. Then I asked who, among the CEOs, wanted to find more cash to grow their business. Of course, they all raised their hands. Even though most of them hadn't done this kind of analysis before, they all had a start on it by the end of the session, and they could already see its value, as well as the value of reviewing it regularly. They were able to see the opportunities to shorten their cycle, correct mistakes, and improve their business model, which all leads to getting cash in hand to grow a business.

We'll talk more about this in Chapter 8, but for now, the best way to start is to take a bottom-up approach. Instead of writing down your revenue and your expenses and figuring out the profit, write down what you want your profit to be month over month and then work your way back. Ask yourself, 'If I want this much profit, what do I need my expenses and revenue to be?' I like thinking of it this way because if you don't write down the profit you want, how can you expect to get it?

These views of your financials are equally important for start-ups and for companies that have been around for a long time. Either way, you still want to grow. And to do that, you have to have a good understanding of your cash, people, and the environment you are playing in.

ACTION ITEMS

1. Download from www.gazelles.com and fill out a FACe chart, with your team, to get clarity on the different roles in your business, metrics, and who is accountable for results in each area.

2. Ask yourself if you would enthusiastically rehire everyone on your team. If the answer is no, this must be addressed.

3. Create an environment map—'The Map'. Do it yourself, first, and then do it with your team, showing all the different players in your 'sandbox'. Look for opportunities to improve your position in your market.

4. Go to the website www.gazelles.com and download and fill out Verne Harnish's Cash Acceleration Strategies (CASh) Worksheet to identify the low-hanging fruit.

5. With your leadership team, draw a cash conversion flow chart to get a clear, detailed picture of how long it takes to go from a sales lead to cash in hand. Look for opportunities to shorten the cycle so you have more cash to use for growth.

CHAPTER 3

CORE PURPOSE, CORE VALUES, AND THE BIG HAIRY AUDACIOUS GOAL (BHAG™)

The best leaders and the best companies make culture their number-one priority. This is fully supported in Jim Collins's study of the most successful companies. You must know your own core purpose and that of your organization. You must know the core values of your team and organization, and you must set a bold goal that lets people see the future they're driving towards. This ensures that your team members have clarity to make excellent long-term-growth decisions on a daily basis.

I recently heard the CEO of Zappos, Tony Hsieh, speak about his top priority, which is to ensure that he has created a culture where he can be successful. This means creating a culture that is a clear and definite one, in which other people know what to expect and can see themselves being engaged and successful as well. That resonated with me because one of the reasons I started both my businesses was to work in an environment where I could grow and be engaged every day. I also wanted to work with people who shared the same values and beliefs. If you have a team who believe in the core values, love the environment and culture that they're a part of, and are clear on where the organization is going, you will have a high-performing team for whatever you set out to do.

Of course, I wasn't fully aware of all this when I started my first company, Paradata. In our early years, a strong culture was something that was implied but not always clear or front and centre among our priorities. We thought it would just happen. In 1999 we were growing very quickly, from four to eighty people in a short period of time, and in turn, we were making a lot of hiring mistakes. I finally asked my team why they thought we were making those mistakes. The reasons came back: because we're hiring a lot of people at once, because we're going a million miles an hour, because there are not a lot of talented people around.

I said, 'Those are all good reasons, but why do you think we hired someone in a development role, who had all the skills we needed, but it was still a mistake? What is the mistake we made?'

We talked about it quite a bit, and finally, we came up with the reason. The person we had employed wasn't a good fit for the team.

Around that time, I read *The Four Obsessions of an Extraordinary Executive* by Patrick Lencioni, which pointed out the need to be clear, both with your existing team and in your hiring practices, and about the core values of your team. We had created a strong culture but were not up front and clear about the fact that we were looking, first, for people who fit our culture—people who shared the same core values—and second, for people with the skills required for the position.

We took Lencioni's message and worked to come up with a clear core purpose and core values for the organization. We got the entire leadership team behind these key elements and then went out to all our offices across Canada, the United States, and Europe to make them known.

In our next monthly 'all-hands' meeting, we spent time defining very clearly why we existed and what our core values were. I knew, as I looked out over the audience, that there were people out there who did not share our views. My executive team asked what we were going to do about that, and I said, 'Two things are likely to happen: Those people will either extract themselves, because they already know they don't fit, or we will have to take action ourselves. We have to be prepared for the consequences of our beliefs because, if these are the things we truly believe, we have to be willing to accept a financial loss over them.'

The next day, two people resigned. We were that clear about our beliefs. There was one person we had to terminate, but that person understood and was actually relieved. All the discussions we had from that point forward about why we should hire someone, why someone shouldn't be on the team, or why we should reward someone, centred on our core values, the key elements that defined our company culture. We had to ensure we were living our core values every day.

CORE PURPOSE

A key part of your culture is your company's core purpose. You must be very clear and your team must be very clear about why your company exists. There are great examples out there of clear and compelling core purposes. 3M's purpose is innovation. Disney's is happiness. When I think about my two companies, in both cases, our purpose was to create an organization that shareholders and team members would value.

I believe, though some people differ on this, that the company's 'why', or core purpose, must be very tight with the leader's 'why', which we talked about in Chapter 1. You usually see this kind of close alignment in companies in their early stage. But in other cases, the core purpose is more in line with what the company does. That is how it often is in companies where the founders are long gone and the leaders have changed multiple times, such as 3M or Disney. There's no right or wrong answer here, but what's essential is that all the people involved believe in the core purpose of the organization. And for that to happen, everybody needs to know what it is.

A lot of people hear this and ask, 'Why does everyone need to know?' There are many reasons, but the most significant is that companies where all the employees know their core purpose and core values—which we'll talk more about in the next section—have a strong culture, which is the foundation for growth and predicting profit. A lot of companies don't spend enough time on this. Jim Collins's research has shown that the most successful companies conscientiously and regularly spend time on their culture, and that is what has kept them successful, even through the worst markets.

SETTING THE BEAT

ORGANIZATIONAL CORE PURPOSE

1. Why do we exist as a business?

2. Test your Organizational Core Purpose by answering the following questions:

YES	NO	Do you find this purpose personally inspiring?
YES	NO	Can you envision this purpose being as valid 100 years from now as it is today?
YES	NO	Does the purpose help you think expansively about the long-term possibilities and range of activities the organization can consider over the next 100 years, beyond its current products, services, markets, industries and strategies?
YES	NO	Does this purpose help you to decide what activities *not* to pursue, to eliminate from consideration?
YES	NO	Is this purpose *authentic*—something true to what the organization is all about—not merely words on paper that "sound nice"?
YES	NO	Would this purpose be greeted with enthusiasm rather than cynicism by a broad base of people in the organization?
YES	NO	When telling your children and/or other loved ones what you do for a living, would you feel proud in describing your work in terms of this purpose?

Acknowledgement: Adapted from JimCollins.com — Vision Framework

Core purposes can evolve, which is why it's important to review them regularly. This can mean little more than putting up a slide during your quarterly meetings or sharing it at monthly 'all-hands' meetings and asking, 'Do we still believe this?' If the answer is no, then action is required.

The leader should present and confirm the organization's core purpose at least **every quarter**.

CORE VALUES

Core values are one of the most misunderstood areas of a company. Core values represent the values of the leader that are shared with the team. A team with strong core values is one in which the members understand their own personal, core values, and are aware of how they fit into the team and into the team's core values.

When I read Patrick Lencioni's book *The Four Obsessions of an Extraordinary Executive*, I adapted from it the initial idea for my core values. Then I worked with my team to define them and make them more personal. We called our core values the three Hs (3H's), rather than Patrick's four Hs, and they were: Happy to come to work, happy to leave; Hungry enough to make a difference; and Humble enough to want to learn every day. Those are my core values and the core values of both the companies I cofounded.

They aren't altruistic values, but they nailed what I was about. And when I shared them with my leadership team, I knew there wasn't a single person who didn't believe in them as well. I hired these people because they believed the same things I did. In fact, many of the team members from my first company joined me in my second company because we shared the same core values. They understood the Metronome Effect methodology, which gave them the opportunity to grow themselves along with the company. The following tools will help you become more aware of your individual values and clear on your team's core values. Those values might even be the same.

setting the beat

> To explore clarifying your organizational core values— download the Organizational Core Values worksheet at www.metronome-effect.com
>
> The leader should present and confirm the organization's core values at least every quarter.

REINFORCING OUR CULTURE

Once I realized that I, as Paradata's CEO, needed to make our culture my priority, we did a number of things to underscore the importance of our core purpose and values:

1. We worked into our hiring practices and human systems ways to discover if candidates shared our core values. First, you have to make sure the candidates have the same core values as the team. Then you can look to see if their skill set is what you need. If their core values do not match, you don't go any further. We realized how important this was after we analyzed the cases of people who hadn't done well after they'd been hired. It became apparent that we were more successful if, somewhere along the way, I'd had a thirty-minute conversation with the candidate. I'd really just wanted to meet the people we were hiring, but in some cases I did speak up to say I didn't recommend that person for various reasons, which always came down to core values. The team wanted to know what I asked people, so I listed some of the questions I asked to really understand if someone was a good fit. After that, we came up with formal

questions that we would ask all the candidates to help identify whether they shared our core values, without telling them what those core values were.

Example of Core Value Interview Questions		
Happy	Hungry	Humble
1. Describe what a 'good' day is for you. 2. What frustrates you? 3. If I called your current/previous immediate supervisor, what would s/he say about you?	1. Describe an experience where you didn't have enough work to keep you busy. What did you do? Describe a time when you had too much work to do in the allotted time. What did you do? 2. What are the three most likely things that would make you change your employment? 3. What are your long-term goals and what are you doing to achieve them?	1. Where do you derive your confidence from? 2. Tell me about a time at work when you had to do something you didn't want to do? How did you handle it? 3. Tell me about a time when you felt you did not receive recognition that was due to you? What did you do about it? Would you do the same again?

2. On Verne Harnish's One Page Plan (OPP), which we'll talk about in Chapter 7, the first two columns provide sections to succinctly write down your core values and purpose. Doing this helps keep the core values and purpose front and centre every

day, week, month, quarter, and year. The OPP is a practical foundational tool for any organization.

3. In our monthly 'all-hands' meetings, we recognized people who oozed and lived our core values daily. Peer recognition was most important in this area. Anybody could recognize other team members during these meetings, which made it fun. People loved it when someone from the implementation team praised someone from the development team; when someone from the development team gave a thumbs up to someone from customer service. This was a way to generate a recognition system around our core values and really show that they were important.

4. Not only did we hire based on our core values, but we fired based on them as well. The core values must be that important. We would have taken a money loss if people hadn't been true to our core values. That's how you know they are truly core values.

 SETTING THE BEAT

Confirm your core values with your team and with the organization as a whole **every quarter**. Do this regularly in case something changes, but also do it to ensure there's clarity around the culture and to reinforce the importance of core values.

BIG HAIRY AUDACIOUS GOAL™

In *Built to Last*, Jim Collins and Jerry Porras coined and trademarked the phrase, *Big Hairy Audacious Goal*, or BHAG. Every company, big or small, should have a BHAG. The most significant reason being that your BHAG, coupled with your core purpose and core values, is the true basis of connecting your culture to your strategy. I recently coached leaders at a company that has been around for about ten years with annual profits in the $10 million range. They wanted me to work with them on strategy. I said, 'Great, but here's where I recommend we start on strategy. I always start with your core purpose and values, and then move to your Big Hairy Audacious Goal, looking ten to twenty years out.'

Your BHAG is a specific goal you're driving the company towards. It has got to be something big, something that makes people uncomfortable, but also something that they can truly see and imagine attaining. I call it 'swinging for the fence'. This is what a home run would look like in your organization. In the first chapter in this book, we talked about the 'why' of the leader and about painting a picture of what that looks like for other team members. Here we're doing something similar. You should be able to describe your Big Hairy Audacious Goal in a memorable, powerful sentence. This sentence must be meaningful enough to be the guiding North Star for the organization. Team members will be making long-term-growth decisions every day based on whether they are heading towards that star.

When we started Paradata, we had a Big Hairy Audacious Goal without even knowing it. The problem with our first and our second BHAGs was that we were swinging for the fence in the wrong markets. We painted a picture, but we quickly realized that we could not generate any revenue in those markets in the near future. But when we came up with our BHAG for the third time, we finally got it right. The point I want to make in telling you this is that, while your core purpose and values probably won't change much over time, your BHAG will.

What happened at Paradata was that we created an encryption system that was one step down from a public key encryption system. We were in the satellite imagery business, and our first goal was to create this system to move data around securely using CD-ROMs. It was a unique piece of technology, but the market changed so quickly that our goal came and went. It was a "big hairy audacious goal" when we started, but the market got deregulated and changed faster than we could. The Internet came along and it became possible to move more data that way. The satellite imagery companies no longer put their data onto CDs.

What came out of that was our second product. We moved our system to the Internet, but then we got ahead of our market. Moving data this way was awfully slow, and there was no way to monetize the product anytime soon.

But, in the process, we realized we had something else that the market valued. When we created our encryption system, we set it up so that in order for a file or CD to be accessed, the customer had to buy the key to unlock the data. We started by manually taking credit card payments by phone, using a credit card machine on our desks. But then, we decided we couldn't have a person answering the phone all the time, so we had to innovate how we took payments. This was the mid-to-late 1990s and e-commerce was the hot trend, so we knew there must be a solution.

We started by looking at all the providers in the marketplace that could be our payment gateway. But the e-commerce hype went well beyond the technology. We figured there must be a tool kit we could use, so we went to IBM and to HP. We got their tool kits and implemented both. In the process, we recognized that banks around the world picked one tool kit or the other. There wasn't one payment gateway that fit all bank processors. So, we had two payment gateways running at the same time. HP and IBM got very excited about what we had done and started introducing us to banks in North America.

Our first call came from a vacation rental property looking to take reservations and process payments over the Internet. I took the call. The caller said, 'We've been referred to you by the Royal Bank of Canada. Would you process our payments?'

I put the phone down and yelled across to my three-person team, 'You guys want to process payments?'

Since we were already processing payments for our own business, they said, 'Sure, let's do that.'

I picked the phone back up again and said, 'I'll send you a contract in about ten minutes.' I went online, found a typical payment gateway contract, changed some info, and sent it over. And that's how our business evolved into an electronic payment service company. Our phone never stopped ringing after that.

So, we evolved one more time, and so did our Big Hairy Audacious Goal. We got very focused on being the leading global payment service provider. Our BHAG was to be the leading global Internet payment service provider for all transactions. This meant that we would support face-to-face transactions as well as transactions that were non-face-to-face. People laughed at us, the banks laughed at us, everybody laughed at us when we said that. At the time, it was hard to believe, because in 1998 nobody knew that the payment infrastructure would be replaced by the Internet.

But we believed it. We knew that there were a lot of infrastructural changes that had to take place before we could meet our BHAG, but we were sure it would all happen in time and we were positioning our company to take advantage of it. When we sold the company in 2006, the platform we set out to create was achieved. It had taken us less than ten years.

When I coach other business leaders and CEOs, I'm often surprised by how many companies don't have a Big Hairy Audacious Goal. If the leader doesn't have one, I ask all the members of the executive team to write down on a sticky note what they think it should be and then stick it on the wall. After that, I call for a break and in between getting some coffee and going to the lavatory, I ask everyone to walk up to the wall and read what people wrote. Then, we look at them together and start grouping ideas. At this stage, I don't really care if the goal is right or wrong. I just want something written down so there is a starting place. Regardless of whether you follow this process or not, you must write down something for your BHAG, or as I call it, 'gut out' a BHAG as a starting place. This BHAG will evolve, but that's OK. This is a journey.

Some time ago I met with another client who nailed his core values and purpose right away, but his BHAG was unfocused. Nobody was really behind it. You could just see it in everyone's body language. The leader asked, 'Why do we need one?' I said, 'That's an excellent question.' I think the answer is obvious, but not everyone sees it.

In the best practices, a BHAG describes which mountain you are climbing. It serves as your North Star. It inherently drives long-term behaviour and guides long-term-growth decisions that must be made every day. If there's no direction or BHAG, what are your team members basing their decisions on? Or are they even making the decisions? Maybe all the decisions are flowing up to the leadership team. A BHAG empowers people to make the best decisions every day for the long-term growth of the company.

I liken it to driving around in a bus. You have your cash in your tank in the form of gas, but you only have so much. Along the way, you might make a little bit of money to pay for more gas, but you'll never know if you've reached your destination if you don't have a destination, or a goal, to begin with. Set out a destination and then work with a team to find the best path forward to reach that destination or goal.

After I explained all this, the client who asked why he needed a BHAG said, 'You know, I just never thought it was important until I started thinking about my team members making decisions on which way we should go when we haven't agreed upon a direction.' He later told me that he spent the next month working nonstop on his BHAG, and when he finally got it and shared it with his team, he could see their eyes light up and a more collaborative discussion began and continued.

BIG HAIRY AUDACIOUS GOAL

| Align | Path | Focus | Energy |

Write from your GUT your BIG HAIRY AUDACIOUS GOAL.

Acknowledgement: 1996 Harvard Business Review published an article, 'Building Your Company's Vision' by Jim Collins and Jerry Porras.

Review your BHAG with your team **every quarter**. Make sure it's still true or decide if it needs to evolve.

OVER-COMMUNICATE THE MESSAGE

In my companies, our core purpose, core values, and BHAG were communicated in many different forms over and over again, starting during the hiring process. I showed slides of all three in every monthly 'all-hands' meeting to the point where people would make fun of how I would present these items. The rhythm of sharing this information happened so regularly that everyone came to expect it, but I kept doing it anyway because I wanted to stay focused on my number-one priority. If this is what we believed in, then we were not going to waiver on these things.

Besides, at every one of those meetings, something had changed—guaranteed. Someone new had joined the team or we'd added a new client. Consistently sharing this information helped everyone stay on track through those changes.

When they'd all heard these things so often that they started making jokes about them, that's when I knew they'd really got it.

ACTION ITEMS

1. Establish a core purpose for the company and compare it to your personal 'why' or core purpose, which you created in the last chapter. Make the company's core purpose known throughout the organization.

2. Establish core values by utilizing the Mars exercise. Make these values known to the team. Integrate them into your human system. Download the Mars Exercise from www.jimcollins.com

3. Even if you're unsure, 'gut it out' and write down a Big Hairy Audacious Goal, something that serves as the company's guiding North Star.

4. Live by your core purpose, core values, and BHAG and make them an integral part of your organization. They should be a key part of your hiring and performance review processes and they should be talked about often. Over-communicate the message!

CHAPTER 4

COMPETITIVE ENVIRONMENT

This chapter is critical for understanding the environment you are competing in. By doing the suggested analysis, you will have a foundation for evaluating your competitive environment for many quarters to come. This analysis is highly effective if done *regularly*. This is the key.

We first talked about your business environment in Chapter 2, when we drew what I call The Map. As my company, Paradata, evolved, we found we needed to map out where our organization fit into the existing market. We were learning about the satellite imagery industry and we needed to understand the external environment and who the players were. Everything was going digital back then, and whenever we thought our product could apply to a new industry— the payments industry, for example—we'd create a new map to give us an overview of that industry. We just did this intuitively.

I create these environment maps in detail now and use them in all sorts of ways. The main reason for their use is to be able to see who has the power in the marketplace and to ensure you put your company in a position of strength. The analysis we'll do in this chapter comes from Professor Michael Porter, an authority on competitive strategy. We will show you how to dive deeper into one aspect of The Map, the forces of an industry. I recommend that you and your leadership team complete a Porter's Five Forces analysis on a regular basis to get a really clear picture of your competitive environment and then go back and overlay what you've learned onto your map.

MICHAEL PORTER'S FIVE FORCES

As I've said before, I've always been an avid reader of business books. When Paradata was in the process of evolving into an electronic payment service company, I came across Michael Porter's Five Forces framework, which wasn't new—it has been around since 1979—but it was new to us. After reading Porter, we created a visual view of the Five Forces framework, which shows who in your industry and marketplace has the power.

Most people, when doing a competitive analysis, look only at their rivals, and most business leaders can tell you that information off the top of their heads. When you ask, 'How are you unique?', they'll know the answer to that, too, saying something like, 'Oh, we beat them on price', or 'We offer this unique feature or function'.

Porter's Five Forces Analysis, which I'll take you through in the coming pages, takes that analysis much further. It's an external analysis of your industry's profitability. Porter uses the example of the airline industry, which is known to have low margins, but there are profitable players that have done very specific things to differentiate themselves. Southwest Airlines and its low-cost position is an example that's cited in both Jim Collins's and Verne Harnish's work.

Porter's framework will help you see what is forcing your environment to do certain things. What we want to do is go through each of the Five Forces one by one and understand where the power lies. Is it with your company or is it with your suppliers, your buyers, new entrants, or your competitors? If all the threats to the industry from these forces are low, the industry will usually have above-normal profits. If all the threats are high, expect normal to below-normal profits. Most industries fall somewhere in between. You aren't likely to see all pluses or all minuses in any category. It's typically a balance.

I sometimes get a negative response from entrepreneurs when I talk about this tool because Porter is a Harvard Business School professor and they think of this tool as an academic template. It is a good practical tool if used on a regular basis, and I've seen it help a lot of companies, including my own and those I currently work with. It's easy and fast, and if you've already created The Map, you and your team can quickly overlay the forces onto it each quarter and compare them to your previous quarter. This quickly gives you a good view of your current position in the marketplace at any one time and supports a good discussion if your position needs to be adjusted.

In the following sections, we'll go through each of the Five Forces one by one so you can do this analysis for your industry. This should be completed with your leadership team. They will have such a varied view of the market, and you want to hear all their perspectives. This is a good way to work with the collaborative mind of your team.

Michael Porter's Five Forces
1. Threat of new entrants
2. Threat of substitute products or services
3. Bargaining power of buyers
4. Bargaining power of suppliers
5. Rivalry among competitors

THREAT OF NEW ENTRANTS

I like to start with the threat of new entrants because in my experience of bringing new technology into established markets, there's always the chance of a new player. Begin by asking yourself and your leadership team how easy it is for others to enter your market.

I once went through this framework with a team from a cement block company, and their answer to this question was 'pretty easy'. Get a dump truck, find a quarry, and off you go. So the threat of new entrants is high for them, but their company is still strong in their market.

Additional questions to ask yourself and your team could include, 'Should newcomers expect sharp retaliation from existing competitors? If you come into the market, what are your competitors going to do?' Write down the answers to these questions with your team and decide together if you think the threat of new entrants is a plus or a minus for your company. Michael Porter created a detailed exercise for each force that I recommend you work with your leadership team to complete. From my experience, this will be a very lively discussion and will provoke a good discussion in an area that most leadership teams are not focusing on.

THREAT OF SUBSTITUTE PRODUCTS OR SERVICES

A good example of the threat of substitute is the cited example in Porter's work of what corn syrup did to the sugar industry, or what Apple's iPod did to the CD player business. The question you're asking yourself and your team is whether there are other products or services that can be easily substituted for yours.

Part of what we were up against at Paradata was the status quo. When it came to processing payments, some people would say, 'No. We'll just keep doing it manually.' They didn't want to adopt a new electronic payment system. That status quo was our substitute. It was mind boggling to us to think of it that way, but doing so helped us get really smart about how we positioned the company and approached the market.

A lot of organizations don't talk about the threat of substitutes on a regular basis. It's not as if you're going to change everything you do because of a potential threat, but you must be aware of whether or not you are in a strong position. When the iPod first came on the market, being a substitute product wasn't a strength for them. It took some time and strategic actions for them to gain a position of strength.

BARGAINING POWER OF BUYERS

The big question here is whether it is easy for buyers to drive down the price. If buyers can drive the price down and it's easy to switch, you do not have a lot of power with your buyers. This happens with cell phone companies, Internet providers, cable TV companies, and the airlines, to name a few examples. There's not a lot of power in those margin businesses.

Our buyers and our competitors had an interesting effect on our power position when I was at Subserveo. In the US market, because we were competing with two companies which charged a lot more than we did—something like twenty times more than what we charged—it drove our price up. We actually had to raise our prices because buyers wouldn't take us seriously if our prices were too low. In the Canadian market, however, there really weren't any other competitors in the marketplace, so the buyers thought our product was too expensive. We could point over the border and say, 'Look at what the solution goes for in the US', but it didn't matter. Being in a market with no competitors really drove our price down.

That happened in part because we were a new product and a new company in the market. Once we put the product in the market—and Subserveo owned the Canadian marketplace for this product—it became so sticky, it wouldn't come out. Because of that, even though we weren't in a position of power in the beginning, we certainly found ourselves in a power position overtime.

BARGAINING POWER OF SUPPLIERS

Do you have multiple suppliers? If you don't, it's very easy for your supplier to drive your price up. If you have a number of suppliers, you're going to hold a bit more power. The fewer the choices, the less power you have.

In that cement block company I was working with, it was easy to pull out the company's map and see what the situation was. The company didn't have a lot of suppliers, but the main supplier was a sister company. The company actually had good amount of power in the industry because of that relationship.

It really controlled its supply chain, and that was such a powerful situation that we gave it two pluses on the company's worksheet. Beyond that, the company delivering the cement was a sister company as well. The owner of this group of companies owned the whole chain. That's pretty powerful.

RIVALRY AMONG COMPETITORS

The last area to look at in the Five Forces framework is the area that most people look at first (and often, it's the only thing they look at). Most business leaders can instantly name their competitors.

One of the things you want to ask yourself and your team here is, 'How intense is the rivalry among the firms we compete with? If we do X, do they respond? Or if they do Y, do we have to respond? How much activity is taking place because of our rivalries?'

In the early days of Subserveo, we had two competitors that were big guns compared to our start-up. In the beginning we were really vague about where we played in market. We originally competed against these two companies for business, even though we didn't believe we could win the business. Nor did we think we should have the business, because it probably would have broken us. It would have been more than we could handle at the time.

Still, we played against those big competitors for about six to twelve months. That helped us get to know them and see what they were about. We realized then that they weren't actually competitors. We did the same things, but in two different market segments. The core customer was different.

If we had continued to compete with them in their segment for the large and extra-large customers, Subserveo probably wouldn't exist today. We understood that they were going to react to us when we competed against them and they would come out swinging. That made us really focus on where we could be most successful in the market. We saw that 80 percent of the market was left to be won with the smaller and midsize businesses, so that's where we positioned ourselves to play.

Those big competitors couldn't respond to the lower price points we were offering these smaller businesses, so they ended up just letting us have that segment of the market. We created momentum with those small- to medium-sized businesses and eventually grew into their segments of large- to extra-large companies. Just before I left the company, we had finally won an extra-large customer. This took five years of growth.

I share that story because the analysis we did of this rivalry helped us find a way to play with these big competitors. We focused on the small- to medium-sized companies for years until we got to the point where we were big enough and profitable enough to go up market and 'play' with these established companies.

We came up with that strategy because we knew our competitors inside and out. Additional questions to ask yourself and your team include, 'How many competitors are there? What are their capabilities? Do they offer equally attractive products or services? How can we do things differently?' At Subserveo, our key activities were very different from those of our established competitors, and that gave us a very powerful position to leverage.

WHAT'S YOUR POWER POSITION?

Once you and your team assess whether you have a plus or a minus in all five areas, you should be able to look at that piece of paper and see how much power you hold in your competitive environment. If you find yourself saying, 'Hmm. I've got five minuses', then you might want to consider if you're in the right business.

Most industries, as I said, will be somewhere in the middle: three pluses and two minuses or three minuses and two pluses. The great news is that once you can see who holds the power in your industry, you can start changing some of your key actions to gain power. To be powerful in an industry, you must assess the market and establish a set of differentiating actions that work together to drive your profit.

At Subserveo we were getting data from suppliers with whom we had no formal agreements. The suppliers could turn that data off at any time, and if they did, we would be out of business. We were very aware of who held the power in this situation, and we organized ourselves to be very respectful of that power. Sometimes you can't change a minus to a plus, but you can still be very aware of the weakness and build around it.

Put up your map and walk through your Five Forces analysis every quarter with your team. It shouldn't take very long once you have completed your first analysis. Each quarter after the first, you just need to assess the changes and adjust for them. And it gets faster and faster each time.

Once we had this down and it was part of our regular rhythm, I used to ask my executive team to show up for quarterly meetings with their analysis already done. Then it took us about five minutes to run through it. You're really looking for the things that have changed since the last time—somebody got bought, some supply became scarce, somebody went out of business, someone new came into the market. I also encourage people to do a new analysis when they bring new products to market. This is an ongoing evolution, a journey you go on to assess where the power is in your marketplace.

SETTING THE BEAT

Review the Five Forces with your team **every quarter** because your environment is constantly changing. The supply of a certain good may become scarce or a new product might enter the market. When you know how the forces are affecting you, you can control some things by changing your minuses to pluses. Download the full Five Forces Worksheet from www.metronome-effect.com.

SHOW YOUR FIVE FORCES POWER POSITION

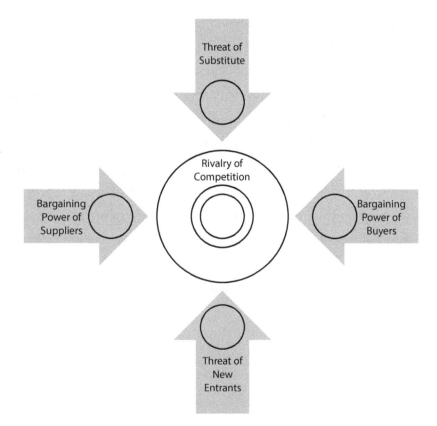

THE ACTIVITY MAP: DIFFERENTIATING ACTIVITIES

Now that you have a clear sense of your power position within your market, we need to create a picture showing the activities that differentiate you from your competitors. Michael Porter and Jim Collins call this an activity fit map, but I just call it an activity map. Both Jim Collins and Michael Porter use an activity map when analyzing companies. See examples at the end of this chapter. What we're doing now is identifying the key activities you have chosen to do that are different from your competitors—a set of activities that your company delivers which differentiate you from your competitors and are the reason why customers buy from you at a profit. This gets at how you have positioned yourself. You've positioned yourself in your industry in a certain way, so let's be clear on the activities that support that.

I'll use the same example of Southwest Airlines that so many others have used. This is a low-value, low-cost airline that chooses certain activities that help it to be a profitable low-value, low-cost airline. These include short-haul trips into midsize cities or secondary airports, like Midway in Chicago, frequent departures, and automated ticketing. The same 737s are used for all their routes. There have been changes at Southwest over time, but that's basically how it came into the marketplace and became the most profitable airline in that marketplace. The company differentiated itself by keeping prices low and offering no frills.

By contrast, the full-service airlines fly everywhere. They have many classes of service and lots of frills like the transfer of baggage and meals. They go to all major airports and have less frequent departures. They use travel agents. They use all types of planes.

Porter, in his *Harvard Business Review* article, 'The Five Competitive Forces that Shape Strategy' (January 2008), cites Singapore Airlines as an example of a top airline with a high class of service. Southwest was on the other end of the spectrum. At one point, Continental came in and tried to straddle both positions, trying to be both low value/low cost and high value/high cost. The airline tried to be too many things for too many people, and what happened was that the CEO lost his job and the company was bought by another airline.

You've got to get very specific about how you position your organization within your marketplace. You've got to be able to say, 'No, we don't do that.' Southwest said, 'No, we're not going to fly everywhere. No, we're not going to offer more than one class of service. No, we're not going to transfer your bags. No, we're not going to charge you for your checked bags.' The company made some very specific decisions. It's all about making trade-offs.

At this point in the book, we've got all these internal and external maps or pictures of our organization. What I like to do now is encourage leaders to write down what they think are their differentiated activities, the areas where they've made trade-offs. Get your executive team to do this as well. Your activity map will, basically, be a page with a bunch of circles. There are bigger circles, which are the key differentiated actions, and then there are a bunch of smaller circles, which are the activities that support these larger actions. It ends up looking like spaghetti with meatballs.

When you do this as a group, you can write the activities on sticky notes and put them up on the wall. Start grouping things together to find your key activities. You might find that there aren't any key activities that differentiate you from your competitors.

MICHAEL PORTER'S EXAMPLE OF
SOUTHWEST ACTIVITY MAP

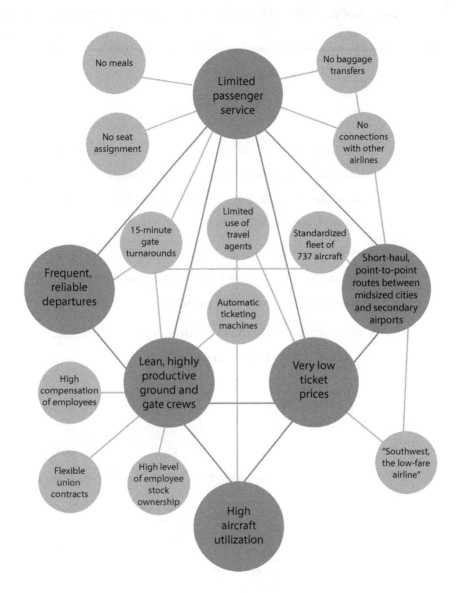

SETTING THE BEAT

Review and update your activity map with your team **every quarter**.

ACTION ITEMS

1. Work through Michael Porter's Five Forces framework as a team and fill out his Analysis Worksheet to see where the power lies in your industry. Download the worksheet at www.metronome-effect.com.

2. Review the results of your Five Forces analysis as a team and compare or overlay it on your map. Look for opportunities to turn your minuses into pluses.

3. Create an Activity Map which shows which activities differentiate you from your competitors.

CHAPTER 5

THE BUSINESS MODEL CANVAS

In the previous chapters on our journey, we've looked at the leader. We've looked at our cash, our team, and our foundation for growth. We've talked about culture and the core purpose and values of our organization. We've become very aware of the environment surrounding us. What we want to do now is put all these puzzle pieces together so we can see where the profitability lies: where it is today and what we can do differently to create more profitability in the future.

Alexander Osterwalder's book *Business Model Generation* came out when I was with Subserveo, and we started using the Business Model Canvas (BMC) tool immediately. We were drawn to it right away because it's visual, and it's something you can build on each quarter.

Everything we've done to this point is identified in the BMC. What this tool allows you to do is write it all down on one piece of paper. I use the tool to visually take everything we identified in our map, in our analysis of the Five Forces, in our cash conversion flow chart, in our Activity Map, and pull all those things together to identify your key stakeholders. The tool lays out nine key areas for analysis: (a) value proposition, (b) key activities, (c) key partners, (d) key resources, (e) customer relationships, (f) customer segments, (g) channels, (h) cost structure, and (i) revenue.

POSITIONING STATEMENT

Before we start filling out our BMC, I like to take a step back and ensure there is clarity around the positioning statement for your company. We've done all this work to date to figure out where we fit in the market, what our environment looks like externally, and what we look like internally, so I now want to be able to have all that reflected in a positioning statement.

I use a simple template that Geoffrey Moore shared in his book *Crossing the Chasm* to create a positioning statement. Whether yours is a new company or an old company, whether or not you have new products going into the market—especially if you have new products going to market—you can use this tool, which is, basically, a table that forces you to write down your positioning statement in one sentence. It asks you to fill in the blanks, which will create a sentence for your positioning statement, which you should articulate in seventeen seconds or less. It's a true elevator pitch. It probably breaks every rule of grammar, but it works.

A good positioning statement will do the following: (a) address the buyer's pain, which is what is needed for the buyer to be motivated to start the buying process; (b) show enough value to have the buyer consider your offering; and (c) differentiate you enough to win the buyer's business.

A few years back, a group of team members from Subserveo attended a conference. It was an invitation-only conference and we hadn't been invited, so we had to go with one of our partners, under that partner's name. We really wanted to be at this conference because the company hosting it was a targeted strategic partner. The conference was held at a hotel and one of my colleagues was getting in the elevator when a gentleman followed him in. He was the CEO of the company that was putting on the conference. He was exactly the person we wanted to talk to.

The CEO turned to my colleague and said, 'How do you like the conference?' My colleague said it was great. Then the CEO asked, 'What do you do?' My colleague was nervous because the team had, basically, snuck into this conference to meet this person, and now he literally had an elevator ride's worth of time to get his attention. So, he used our positioning statement. When they got to the CEO's floor, the doors opened and the CEO said to my colleague, 'Would you mind stepping off the elevator so we can talk more about this?' This company ended up becoming a key strategic partner after that. Your positioning statement must immediately resonate!

I like to tell that story because I've heard a lot of people say that the positioning statement is too academic. Well, it doesn't have to be. The whole idea behind your positioning statement is to capture the attention of your target audience. If you position yourself well, they'll understand who you are and why you're important to them and that should leave a place in their minds for you.

A strong positioning statement takes time to get right. In the very beginning, we would create a positioning statement for our new product and try it out on different people. We would then tweak it until we could really see the 'twinkle' in their eye that said, 'Yes. Wow, we want to know more about that.' We were pretty confident in our positioning statement by the time that CEO got in the elevator with my colleague. He didn't expect the CEO to ask him to step off the elevator to talk more about it right then and there, but we knew it was solid.

That positioning statement worked so well that I can remember meeting with target customers in the first year of our business, and, four years later, getting calls from some of them. They hadn't been ready to buy from us when we first talked, but they remembered us and called back. That's exactly what you want a positioning statement to do: occupy a space in the mind of those people you're talking to so they think of you when they're ready to do business, when they need what you have to solve their problem and pay for it at a profitable level.

Geoffrey Moore's Positioning Statement Template	
For	(specifically describe target customer)
Who	(statement of need or opportunity)
The (product name) is a	(product category)
That	(statement of key benefit—that is compelling reason to buy)
Unlike	(competitors or primary competitive alternative)
Our product	(statement of primary differentiation)

Note: This should take no more than 30 seconds to say— target 17 seconds.

THE VALUE PROPOSITION

Why start with a positioning statement when we're talking about the BMC? Because your value proposition, which is the centre box on your BMC, is founded on your positioning statement. Again, we used a Geoffrey Moore template for supporting the creation of our valuation proposition. Four of the six lines in your positioning statement have the same answers as four of the six lines in your value proposition. The difference is that with your value proposition, you want to gain attention—from your buyer, your partner, or from whomever you need the attention—by showing that your differentiated value is superior to that of your competitor's differentiated value.

My recommendation is to create or confirm your value proposition before filling out the rest of your Business Model Canvas, because it's the only step we haven't touched on in this book so far. To fill in the remaining eight sections, you can simply pull from the tools we've already used.

In *The Business Model Generation*, Osterwalder takes a different approach. Both ways are valid. The one I've described is one that works with the regular rhythm of the Metronome Effect methodology.

We have worked through the fundamentals in each of the steps we've taken to this point, but we have yet to test our value proposition. Starting with it here reminds the leadership team to spend worthwhile time to create a strong value proposition for their customer segments. They can build on the pieces we've already worked through to do this. In the last chapter, we looked at our external environment, which sets up the foundation for our positioning. And once we have created a positioning statement, it's a lot easier to come up with our value proposition. And once we have our value proposition, we can start filling in our BMC.

Geoffrey Moore's Value Proposition Template	
We Believe that	(Target Company Buyer) Line 1 of PS (For)
Should be able to	(Positive impact on critical business issues addressed) Line 2 of PS (Who)
By	(Specific measurement or KPI, #, $, %)
Through the Ability to	(Specific action you enable) Line 4 of PS (That Provides)
As a result of	(Your unique differentiated capabilities) Line 6 of PS (Our Product)
For an investment of approximately	(Average deal $$ estimated)

FILLING OUT THE REST OF THE BMC

The Business Model Canvas pulls together all sorts of tools from various thought leaders. The information we get from business books and other sources tends to be very siloed. What this tool does, and what Metronome Effect methodology does in general, is help you to put all that wisdom and information together in one place so you can get a superior view of your business.

Most companies already have a forecast, their financials, and a month-over-month plan. They might be profitable or they might not be there yet, but either way, this tool brings your economic engine into the picture—not in an Excel spreadsheet, but in a way that's easy to visualize.

The best practices suggest a very specific SWOT analysis of this particular tool, before you even start filling it out. I actually don't use that part of this tool. (We will, however, do a SWOT analysis later on, as part of our OPP in Chapter 7.) Instead, I pull out the tools we've already produced in the first four chapters and start plugging in the information.

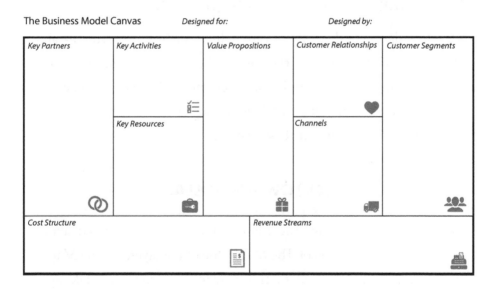

KEY ACTIVITIES

Guess what? When we did our Activity Map, we already noted our key activities.

KEY RESOURCES

We have identified key resources and the power of our key resources when we walked through Porter's Five Forces. You can also identify these from The Map.

KEY PARTNERS

We've already identified our key partners on our map.

CUSTOMER SEGMENTS, CUSTOMER RELATIONSHIPS, AND CHANNELS

To fill out the remaining three boxes in the top section of the BMC, you can again refer back to The Map we created in Chapter 2.

COST STRUCTURE AND REVENUE STREAMS

The foundation of the BMC is cash, which is why Cost Structure and Revenue Streams appear at the bottom. Here's where we look at how much money we take in and how much money is going out as a way to monitor whether you are making money or not. Read on for more information on filling out these two sections.

FOLLOW THE DOLLAR

When we talked about The Map in Chapter 2, we talked about creating different layers of The Map. One of the layers of The Map is what I call 'follow the dollar'. This view follows how you're taking in cash and who is delivering cash to your company, by connecting the boxes that represent your relationships. I usually colour the connected lines green because green is the colour of cash. And I usually include percentages to show where the biggest dollars are coming from. Once you do this, you can see your revenue streams, which plug directly into the bottom right section of the BMC.

Then, if you look at the back end of The Map, where we have all our suppliers—where we have costs—I link those up to my company and again colour them green and show the percentages. Sometimes people will colour the costs in red because they represent money going out. The purpose of following the dollar is to track where it starts, which is with customers, and where it goes. In my case, some of it stays within my organization and some of it leaves in order to pay for my supplies and my suppliers.

We then take those costs from The Map and put them in the Cost Structure box on the lower left-hand side of the BMC. (There's actually an iPad app you can use to do this. You can put in your revenue streams and your costs and it kicks out your profit margins. You can find this iPad App at http://www.businessmodelgeneration. com/toolbox/bmtbox.)

A SIMPLE VIEW

One of the things I love about Osterwalder's book Business Model Generation is that he took all of these pictures of the business and integrated the financial piece, so it's a business model and a business plan. These things are often long, forty-page documents, but he brings it all together in a single-page view of the business model, the financial analysis, and the external environment. Once you have this, you can start thinking about your execution.

What I recommend when creating a BMC is that you work through every step with your team. I like to take a generic template (see the end of this chapter for an example) and blow it up on a big piece of paper or on a large whiteboard. Then, we fill in the boxes together, using sticky notes. I love the fact that this tool can be interactive and unlock the collaborative mind of the team. Make reviewing this tool part of your quarterly rhythm.

One of the questions I'm often asked is how I fit this in every ninety days. After four quarters of doing this every ninety days with your team, your team will show up prepared, and you will go faster. Once you have a handle on it, you're just looking at what has changed, not creating the canvas from scratch.

SETTING THE BEAT

The Business Model Canvas is a dynamic tool that should grow with you every day, but at minimum, review it **every quarter.**

Visit www.businessmodelgeneration.com for a BMC template.

ACTION ITEMS

1. Create a positioning statement for your organization. It will take time to get it right, but write something down with your team and then work to pare it down to a seventeen-second statement. Use Geoffrey Moore's template to help you.

2. Next, create your value proposition. Again, use Geoffrey Moore's tool to help you work through this with your team.

3. Work through the Business Model Canvas step by step with your team, using all the tools you've worked through so far to fill it in.

CHAPTER 6

STRATEGIC THINKING

THE PAGE BEHIND THE PAGE

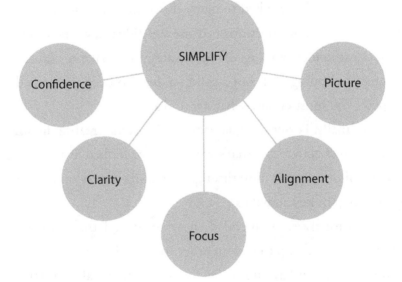

When Verne Harnish's Seven Strata of Strategy came out, it was a much-needed framework that forced you to succinctly write down your strategy. This is the hardest part of strategy: taking something complex and writing it down, simply. I so often encounter leaders who believe they have a strategy but find it hard to write it down. The Seven Strata of Strategy forces you and your leadership team to write down your strategy in simple terms. It's also what I call the page behind your One Page Plan (OPP), which we'll talk about in the next chapter on execution.

Michael Porter's definition of strategy, in his *Harvard Business Review* article, 'What Is Strategy', is 'the creation of a unique and valuable position involving a differentiating set of activities'. The last chapter, with its focus on your position statement and value proposition and all the work you have done to date, has set a solid foundation for you to simply write down your strategy.

Porter also says that strategy requires you to make trade-offs, and this piece of advice is critical. During the first five years of my first business, we were terrible at this. We didn't make trade-offs. We had technology that applied to many different industries and we got pulled in all sorts of directions because we didn't have the discipline or the clear understanding of our strategy to make a choice. We had great technology but not a solid strategy to keep us focused. To compete, you must choose what *not* to do.

And finally, Porter says that strategy involves 'creating fit among the company's activities'. That's why we have looked at the internal activities of our organization through our cash conversion flow chart, and our map of key activities.

It is strongly recommended that you do all the foundational work we've covered up to now in order to move into the Seven Strata of Strategy. (If you have not been able to complete all the steps and want to move forward, continue under the premise of 'gutting out' the answers and the ones where you are stuck are surely where you should go back and review the previous steps.) Two more steps before we can move on:

1. **WHO: Know Your Customer**

   An analysis of your core customer is a key activity to complete now and on a regular basis. Most organizations that I have worked with, or even in my own company early on, did not spend enough time on a detailed analysis of the core customer. We could identify the segment and type of company, but we did not go into enough detail. The recommendation is to do a six-step analysis, based on Robert Bloom's book *Inside Advantage*, to understand your core customer. This will entail describing the core customer right down to the individual, and understanding that individual's online behaviours and greatest needs. To work through the six step adapted worksheet based on Robert Bloom's book *Inside Advantage* go to www. metronome-effect.com.

Six Steps to your Core Customer Based on Robert Bloom's *Inside Advantage*	
GOAL: A statement that clearly illustrates your Core Customer.	
1	Start with a list of your current customers. Add competitor's customers that you currently want as well.
2	Put an asterisk next to customers who are perceived as most valuable.
3	Discuss with your team who would be valuable clients to add to the list.
4.	Who are your highest priority customers? Underline the customers that you want to keep. As well, underline the customers you want to add to your client list.
5	Look at just these high priority customers: a. Define these individuals using two or three specific words or phrases. b. What are their specific individual traits or characteristics? c. Why are they high priority for you? d. What makes them a good fit for your company's culture or specific product/service offering? e. Does the team like working with these customers? Why? f. At this point, just list as much information about the customer as you can, then pull it together in a definition that's about 20 words long. Your definition won't be perfect.
6	Come up with a list of 10-15 things that the Core Customer you've identified desires. Challenge yourselves to live in your customer's shoes and try to see things from their perspective. Collect some insights from those on your team who interact with the customers most often and even from the customers themselves about what they want.

Adapted from Patrick Thean's Blog.

2. Attribution Framework

The Attribution Framework tool is a way to identify and understand the key characteristics of your marketplace and then assess how your organization stacks up against those characteristics compared to your competitors.

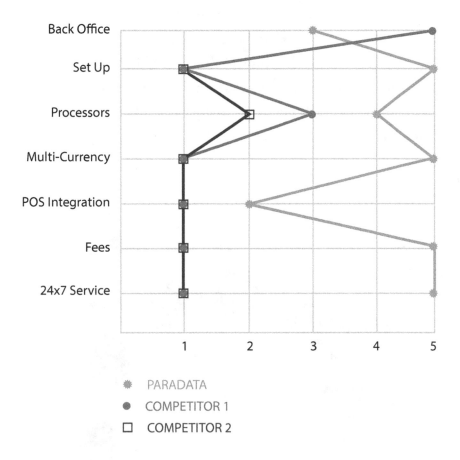

The example above shows Paradata and Competitor 1 and Competitor 2—the latter two serve the large and extra-large customers in this market, and are very similar in their offerings. Paradata entered the market with a software-as-a-service offering, targeting the small to medium customers in the market. The needs of these customers compared to the large and extra-large customers were very different. In order to meet the needs of these customers, Paradata had to focus on unique activities. You can see from the example shown above that we made strong trade-offs to ensure we were serving the greatest needs of our customers.

Create a table as in the example above. Fill in the characteristics/attributes of your market and then rate, on a scale of 1–5, how your organization meets these characteristics. Then map two or three competitors in the same table. This will allow you quickly to see your key differentiating actions, as well as the white space available to position your company in a strong profitable position, based on your core customer.

7 STRATA OF STRATEGY

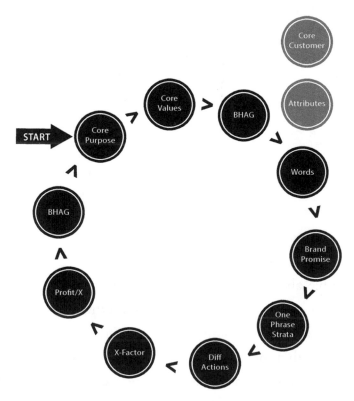

Verne Harnish's Seven Strata of Strategy framework basically comprises seven questions, which we'll go through one by one. The goal is to easily create and simply write down your strategy in order to communicate to all. This is your strategic thinking laid out in a simple step-by-step framework. This strategic thinking maps directly to Column 2 and Column 3 of the One Page Plan (OPP) that is covered in the next chapter.

SEVEN STRATA OF STRATEGY

1. WHAT WORDS DO YOU WANT TO OWN IN YOUR MARKETPLACE?

If someone is searching for you on the Internet, what words will that person enter in a search engine to find you? This is really about mindshare and positioning.

Start by looking at your positioning statement. You may find that answering this question challenges what you have for a positioning statement. It may also challenge what you're doing to be found through the Internet. That's what happened to us at Subserveo. We started out answering the question with very generic words: broker, dealer, compliance. Every quarter we worked to refine these words so we became more and more specific. After about two years, there were certain regulations that our software as a service addressed, and we decided those should be included in the words we owned.

I encourage you to work through this with your executive team. Sit down and brainstorm together. Create a list of words and start narrowing them down from there. Your word list might grow over time because your business grows over time. If you're a big company in five different industries, there can be a different set of words that you own for each industry. You're looking to position the company so that someone who is searching for 'X' will find you.

2. WHAT IS YOUR UNIQUE BRAND PROMISE?

The work we did above in understanding our core customer right down to individuals and their behaviour is directly related to your unique brand promise. We also identified the customers' greatest need. With this in mind, a unique brand promise should be created that really matters to your customer, will attract customers to your organization to buy at a profit, and will differentiate your organization from that of your competitors. With your team, brainstorm brand promises that matter to your core customer. Look at your market and find out if there are any brand promises being made by your competitors. Look at different companies that you might buy from. Do they have a brand promise? This will get a good discussion going in your brainstorm session and really drive home why a brand promise matters. It makes it easier for the customer to buy at a profit.

CHARACTERISTICS OF A UNIQUE BRAND PROMISE

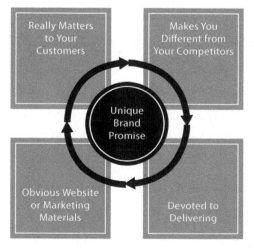

Your #1 Brand Promise should address what you feel is the greatest need
your customer has that you can solve better than your competition.

3. HOW WILL YOU MAKE YOUR BRAND PROMISE HURT?

Once you state your unique brand promise, the next step is to make sure it hurts your company if you don't keep your promise. This should make your team very uncomfortable. This 'hurt' is what Jim Collins calls a catalytic mechanism. This mechanism, by making your brand promise guarantee the 'hurt,' will distribute power to your company. It obtains desired results in unpredictable ways. It will attract the right people to the team and eject the people who do not want the transparency of delivery with known consequences.

My second company, Subserveo, was focused on making post-trade compliance easy for small to medium broker-dealers in North America. We aimed at being a very high-touch, high-service company. To underscore this promise, we assured customers the service level would exceed their expectations, and if it did not, they could cancel at any time.

When I worked through our leadership team brainstorm session, I said, 'Look, I don't want to be a cell phone company where you can't get out of your contract without a penalty, even if you're getting poor service.'

This was putting our money where our mouth is. We were going to provide the service our customer expected or we were going to pay for it if we did not meet their expectations. This meant that the cancel-anytime clause would hurt our organization through the loss of investment we had made to enable the customer to use our platform, as well as the loss of recurring revenue. The promise made our team uncomfortable, and it should make your team uncomfortable. Failing has to hurt internally.

How you make something hurt changes the way your team members think about delivery of the brand promise. I was consulting with a company that had a really bold brand promise and good ways to keep track of whether that promise was being kept. But when I asked what happened if they didn't make good on their promise, the team said nothing happened. So we came up with a way they could make it hurt. I could see the CFO doing the math on his calculator, adding up how much it could cost them if they failed. So, I asked, 'Why will this not come true?' The team said, 'Because we're going to ensure all the internal activities are in place to guarantee we deliver on our promise.' Making it hurt gets your entire team extremely focused on what matters to the customer.

Then I said, 'If you deliver on this promise, what will that do for your business?' They said, 'Everyone will want to buy from us.' That promise allowed them to position themselves differently from their competitors and attract customers to buy at a profit.

To ensure your unique brand promise is right, ask the following questions:

(a) Does it differentiate the company in the marketplace?

(b) Does it really matter to the customer?

(c) Is the company brand promise attracting new customers sales?

(d) Does it align sales and delivery teams internally?

(e) Is it driving decision making in terms of products and service offerings?

4. WHAT'S YOUR ONE-PHRASE STRATEGY?

A lot of CEOs can articulate their strategy, but less than 5 percent can say it in one phrase. That percentage is probably even lower for a leadership team. This can be a tough area for a team to work through, but it needs to be 'gutted out'—just written down and pared down over time.

This one phrase isn't necessarily something that's going to be used externally. It could be a phrase that only means something to your team. In fact, I think it's important to keep it internal, unless there are reasons to share it externally, maybe with investors or a company seeking to buy your organization.

Your one-phrase strategy must support your brand promise. One example I use all the time is from Southwest Airlines. Their one-phrase strategy, for which they are famous, is 'Wheels up' because their goal is to get on the ground, unload the plane, load the plane, and get it back as fast as possible in the air where they're most profitable. Every minute they're on the ground costs Southwest money. Keeping their planes in the air not only generates profit, it also allows them to keep their airfares low for their customers.

Michael Porter's Activity Fit Map of Southwest Airlines, in Chapter 4, shows six key activities that support the airline's one-phrase strategy. We've done the work of drawing our key differentiating activities, so with those, plus your brand promise, work with your team to brainstorm your company's one-phrase strategy.

In both my companies, our strategy was all about data—any data, anywhere, anytime. In my first business, this was about payment data, and in my second company, it was about compliance data. One of the reasons this one-phrase strategy resonated with our team at Subserveo was that our customers told us it was hard to get all their compliance data from their back end systems into one place with an easy, online, information review platform. They had to spend many hours, daily, creating static reports, printing a lot of paper, and reviewing it manually with a highlighter. Subserveo focused on getting, reviewing, and presenting this data in an electronic form, daily, from any system our customers required.

I recommend taking the time with your team to sit down and brainstorm a phrase that resonates. What I suggest, as always, is to write down everything. If you come up with two or three sentences at first, good enough. Write them down and carry on. Then, come back later and keep paring the wording down until all that's left is that one phrase that resonates with your team.

5. HOW WILL YOU SUPPORT YOUR ONE-PHRASE STRATEGY WITH DIFFERENTIATING ACTIONS?

The Attribution Framework that you created in a previous step and your activity map (Porter's Activity Fit Map) from Chapter 4 are key resources for bringing clarity to this step. Review both of these visuals and then write down between three and six differentiating activities that creates your unique position in the marketplace.

In Southwest's case, which Porter uses as an example, the company was very particular about what it picked as its actions, and it's famous for it. The airline made sure it was known as the 'cheap and cheerful airline', and its six key differentiating actions reinforced (a) limited passenger service, (b) frequent, reliable departures, (c) lean, highly productive ground and gate crews, (d) high aircraft utilization, (e) low ticket prices, and (f) short-haul, point-to-point routes between mid-sized cities and secondary airports. All those differentiating activities together—not just one—put Southwest into a unique position and made it the valuable company it is today. Lots of airlines tried to copy just one or two of these actions and failed. Take some time now to get clear on your company's differentiating actions. Once they are clear, then brainstorm with your team the supporting actions of these three to six actions as shown in the Southwest Activity Fit Map.

6. WHAT'S YOUR X-FACTOR?

You've identified your differentiating actions. Now you need figure out what's going to be your X-factor. This is your twofold to tenfold competitive advantage.

In the previous step, we came up with three to six differentiating actions that truly position the company. If a competitor mimics any one of them, that's great, but no competitor should be able to copy all of them. In this step, we're looking for that X-factor, and it is highly recommended to keep the X-factor to your internal team.

In both my companies the X-factor came down to the same thing. It was about mapping data as a way to scale the business. In Paradata we mapped data from all payment processors in Canada, the US, and Europe. This gave us a way to leverage the channels of all these payment processors to scale the customers using the platform. In my second company, we were able to map all our customers' data sources into one platform to provide one consolidated view. By doing this, we were able to leverage the data sources as channels to scale up our customers.

In both these businesses, we became very 'sticky' to our customers. We were integrated into their back office as a critical system. We knew we had achieved what we wanted when customers changed their payment process or clearing firm but did not change our platform in their back office.

Here are some questions to consider to make sure you have the right X-factor:

(a) Does it solve an industry bottleneck?

(b) Does it revolutionize a marketplace?

(c) Will it mature and be copied?

(d) Does it give you a twofold to tenfold advantage in the marketplace?

Once you find your X-factor, never stop looking for the next X-factor. Your X-factor will mature and will be copied. The market will evolve. A great example of this is Blockbuster. That company had a strong X-factor when it came to the deal that was negotiated directly with the studios, which brought the company a tenfold advantage over competitors on cost alone. But Blockbuster got beaten when it did not respond to Netflix's development of the model. Do not get 'fat and happy' with your current X-factor. Always be looking for the next tenfold advantage.

7. MEASURE YOUR PROFIT PER X AND BHAG

Two very crucial decisions: profit per X and your Big Hairy Audacious Goal. These decisions are very tightly coupled. Your profit per X is what drives the economic engine for your business. Your BHAG is to provide a convincing picture and goal for your team that is at least ten years into the future and that will help guide them to make good decisions for long-term growth, daily.

Profit per X is the single most important key performance indicator (KPI) for leaders to track. At Paradata, our profit per X was profit per merchant subscriptions. At Subserveo, it was profit per user. We actually started out measuring revenue per user in the beginning. This view kept me and, in turn, the company very focused on what mattered most to our organization. To find your 'X' in profit per X, look at the fundamental assumption in your business model. Our business was driven by subscriptions. We had to ensure that every subscriber we added was profitable. The core assumption in our business model was subscriptions. What is your core assumption in your business model?

In Chapter 3 you wrote down your BHAG. After all the steps we have taken since then, what we want to do is look at this BHAG and reflect on whether this is the right BHAG. Does it give your team a picture they can believe in? Is it a goal they do not know how to achieve, but they will still buy into driving the company in that direction? And will you know if you get there?

Your BHAG should be very tightly connected to your strategy. That is why we are revisiting it at this time, after working through the key elements of the strategy. Do you need to change your BHAG? My guess is that 50 percent of my clients changed or evolved their BHAG after this analysis. Don't feel you have to change it now if you feel your BHAG is aligned with your strategy. Otherwise, work with your team to develop your BHAG so that it is aligned with your strategy. The most important thing is to 'gut it out'—write something down. Do not leave this blank.

Checklist to consider when creating your BHAG:

1. It should give a picture of the 'mountain you are climbing'.

2. It should serve as your company's North Star.

3. It should drive long-term behaviour.

4. It should ensure decisions are being made with long-term growth in mind.

At Paradata, when we first created a BHAG, we didn't think we needed to put any measurements around it because it looked too far into the future, at least ten to twenty years out. We just wanted to paint that picture in a sentence so that when team members were making decisions, they had at the front of their minds the direction we were going. If, for instance, a developer was deciding how to structure error messages in an interface, he might have done it differently if he had known we were going global in ten years and would need to support twenty languages.

However, I was also taught a long time ago that a goal is not a goal unless it can be measured. One of the things I love about profit per X is it allows you to put a metric on your BHAG without changing the memorable sentence that describes where you're going.

I'll use the example of Southwest Airlines because I've talked about it so many times already. 'Wheels up' is the airline's one-phrase strategy, and I mentioned the actions it took to support that. With that in mind, the airline's profit per X was basically its profit per plane in the air. That totally tied everything together.

Don't be put off if you can't pull out your profit per X right away. Sometimes you need time to work this formula, and that's OK. Write down what you think it might be, and then come back to it after you've worked on your financials in Chapter 8. Eventually it will become clear if you keep working through this framework.

SETTING THE BEAT

Check in with your Seven Strata of Strategy worksheet **every quarter.** Or, if you're new to this or if you've had trouble completing any of the sections, bring it up with your team **every 30 days** until everyone is comfortable with the answers. After that, a quarterly review is all you need. The Seven Strata of Strategy Worksheet can be downloaded from the Gazelles website at www.gazelles.com

SEVEN STRATA OF STRATEGY WORKSHEET

Words You Own (Mindshare)			

Brand Promises			
Who/Where	What	Brand Promises	KPIs

Brand Promise Guarantee (Catalytic Mechanism)

One-PHRASE Strategy (To Pay for Brand Promises)

Activities (3 – 5 Hows)

X-Factor (10x – 100x Underlying Advantage)

BHAG® (10 – 25 Year Goal)	Profit/X (Economic Engine)

Gazelles Growth Tools™ v2 – 1.12   For use by Gazelles International Coaches.
©2012 Gazelles, Inc. BHAG is a Registered Trademark of
Jim Collins and Jerry Porras.

ACTION ITEMS

1. Focus on your core customer by completing the six steps Robert Bloom recommends in his book *Inside Advantage*.

2. Create with your team an attribution framework for your company and specific segments if this applies.

3. Step through each of the seven steps of the Seven Strata Framework with your team. Fill in the worksheet. Every ninety days at least, revisit this work.

CHAPTER 7

EXECUTION

In my work as an executive coach and speaker, I have met a lot of leaders, but I haven't met many leaders who don't have trouble being clear about who should be doing what and when within their organizations. I've worked with more than a hundred companies in a variety of industries, and everyone seems to struggle with accountability, whether they are aware of it or not.

All the things we've done to this point have been building blocks to get us to the stage where we can define our plan, based on Verne Harnish's One Page Plan (OPP). This is the step we take to ensure accountability, by setting up a rhythm for executing our plan.

I love this page because it takes all the work we've done creating all these different pictures of our business and puts them onto one page that I can easily add to the notebook I carry around. I carry all these tools with me wherever I go so that, when I'm having conversations with a customer, a partner, a team member, a shareholder, a board member, or an investor, they serve as my cheat sheets. They make me much more effective as a CEO because they keep me focused and consistent. They are critical in presenting very simply and clearly something as complex as a company strategy and plan.

ONE PAGE PLAN BROKEN DOWN

The One Page Plan (OPP) is really two pages printed as one. I recommend you fill it out from left to right. The first column is about things that will rarely change. They are the reason for the company's existence, the core values, and BHAG, looking ahead (a) more than ten years, (b) three to five years, (c) twelve months, and (d) ninety days. You'll end by writing down what you will hold yourself personally accountable for and what your team will hold you accountable for, both in terms of key performance indicators and your top initiatives for the next ninety days.

As you look at the completed page from right to left, the things you're going to do in the next ninety days should roll up into the corporate ninety-day plan, which should roll into the twelve-month plan, which should roll into the three-year or five-year plan, which should roll into how you're going to set yourself up for the next ten to twenty years.

In this chapter, I'll run through how we did this at both my companies. I suggest you start with a standard version of the plan (see the templates at the end of this chapter), and then, as we've done over the years, you might make some adjustments as you go.

THE ONE PAGE PLAN—THE WATERFALL FOUNTAIN

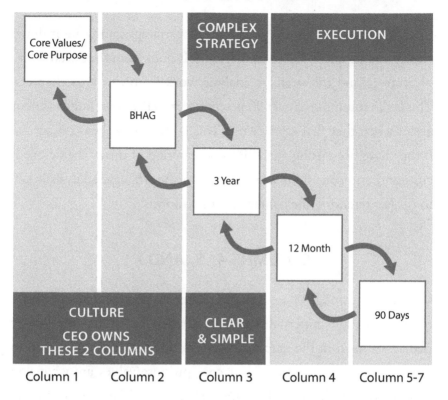

COLUMNS 1 AND 2

The OPP from left to right starts on the very left with column 1, which forces you to write down your core values and your core competencies. Column 2 asks for the company's core purpose, the BHAG, and the key actions the CEO will own in order to ensure the core values, core purpose, and BHAG are being carried out. The CEO owns columns 1 and 2 as these columns represent the culture of the organization. And this is the CEO's number-one initiative.

COLUMN 3

Column 3 is a way to take your complex strategy and write it down clearly and simply for all to understand. It pulls from the Seven Strata of Strategy and the strategic analysis work from previous chapters. This is the column that over 90 percent of my clients are not confident about when they first contact me. This is truly why they contact me if they have been using an OPP for any period of time. The detailed, constant, and consistent work related to the strategic analysis is key to easily presenting the content of this column.

COLUMNS 4, 5, AND 7

Columns 4 through 7 are directly related to the company's twelve-month plan and ninety-day plan, and each individual ninety-day plan. As shown in the graphic, each of these columns are related to the column on either side. Your core purpose/values are what you believe. Your BHAG is where the company will be in ten or more years, which drives to where you need to be in three years, which drives to your twelve-month plan (column 4), which in turn drives to the corporate ninety-day plan (column 5), and then drives to each individual's ninety-day plan (column 7).

COLUMN 6

Column 6 is all about representing and planning the thirteen-week race you will create to make sure the ninety-day plan is focused, fun, and delivered. This provides a way to share with your team a theme to represent the quarter, the key target, and what the reward will be for achieving the quarterly plan.

FILLING OUT YOUR ONE PAGE PLAN

COLUMN 1

Fill in the Core Values in the top section of column 1. The bottom section of column 1 is titled: Core Competencies. We have not yet addressed this. Write down what your firm is great at, which means that these competencies are something that your customers perceive you are very good at. It took years for your organization to build the process and for those handling these competencies to be great at them. Write down one to three core competencies.

COLUMN 2

Fill in your Core Purpose at the top of column 2. The next section is called Key Actions. Since the CEO owns columns 1 and 2, these are the CEO's, or leader's, key actions. What are the five things you are going to do to ensure the organization is living its values and purpose? When I first started to use this section, it took me a few quarters to figure out what my actions as the CEO should be. I found a list of actions that became the foundation of what my focus was as the CEO of my business. Once I wrote these down, they did not change.

These actions are about the leader's commitment and promise to the team to ensure a healthy organization. I would show my five actions at the monthly 'all-hands' meetings and at every quarterly meeting with my team. I did this to demonstrate my commitment to ensuring that everyone knew my key initiative was to make the company culture a priority.

The key actions that all CEOs should make their priorities—to ensure the strong health of the organization—came from reading

Patrick Lencioni's second book, *The Four Obsessions of an Extraordinary Executive*, and they are as follows:

1. **Consistent human system:** The CEO is accountable for ensuring there is a strong process for hiring the right people, growing the right people, rewarding them, and removing the wrong people. That was my responsibility, not HR's, which definitely supported me. I needed to make sure we had a consistent human system that ensured we were living by our values and that we were hiring, firing, and rewarding based on those values.

2. **Team cohesiveness:** As CEO, I was accountable for making sure my executive team was cohesive and that my team leaders had the tools they needed to make their own teams cohesive. (We will talk more about this in Chapter 9.)

3. **Consistent messaging:** The OPP and the consistent use of this throughout our companies supported this discipline.

4. **Clarity:** This came in the form of making sure there was a constant communication system based on the OPP in place at the company, starting with the daily, weekly, monthly, 'all-hands', quarterly, and annual meetings and weekly email status updates. This was my opportunity to regularly drive home the key messages of the company.

5. **Over-communicate clarity:** The CEO must make sure that the key messages are communicated in many different ways and forms at least seven times for each message. This was my responsibility.

To complete column 2, write down you profit per X and BHAG in the bottom sections of this column. These comprise the foundation of the team you lead. It is important to get these two columns as clear as possible as soon as possible.

COLUMN 3

This column is one of the most important columns in the plan and the least understood. It is where you write down your complex strategy in simple and clear terms. At the top of this column is the subhead, 'Targets (3–5 Years)'. I strongly recommend this column be titled, 'Targets (3 Years)'. Three years is close enough to know how to get there with some certainty. It is easy to build out a thirty-six-month forecast. This column will provide your team with a good picture of three years out.

At the top of this column is a table for the financial number three years out. Write down the 'year ending' that is three years away. For example, if the year we are in is 2014, then I'm looking at the year ending three years from now and I'm writing down '31 December 2017'. Then the question is what the financial critical numbers will be in three years.

My recommended process is to fill out your OPP with your team first, and then create a thirty-six-month forecast that supports the plan. Then you can easily insert the financial targets for three years out.

In Verne Harnish's template, the numbers suggested are revenues, profit, and market cap. The critical financial numbers should be what best provides a picture to your team as to where you will end up in three years time. I suggest you don't write down market cap, especially if your company is young. I think that number can get you into a bit of trouble. It's more important to write down your revenues, expenses, and profit—especially profit. If you're going to grow your profit, you've got to write down a number for it.

As mentioned above, the specific numbers to be inserted here are from the thirty-six-month, month-over-month plan that you should build from the bottom up with your team. If, at this point, you don't have a thirty-six-month plan—and I've worked with a lot of companies that don't—that's OK. Come up with what you think the critical numbers might be in three years. Estimate a range. And if you can't even guess at them right now, no big deal. Go off and do your homework on your financials to forecast your profit (see the next chapter for more on this), expenses, and revenues, and then fill in the table at the top of column 3.

The next step is to work with your team to describe where you want to play in three years. This is what Verne Harnish calls your 'sandbox'. There are a few ways to approach this. Verne Harnish suggests the team answers these three questions: Where will you sell? What will you sell? Whom will you sell to? The other approach is to come up with a sentence that describes what your company will be in three years. For example, at Subserveo, we wanted to be the North American leader for post-trade compliance solutions.

The idea is to think of where you want to be ten years out and then work backwards to figure out what you need to accomplish in three years. It is vitally important to get the whole team's belief in the BHAG and then play in the sandbox. Be specific and write down a goal here. It could be 'to own 20 percent of the North American market'. That's something the team can get behind. When people have a target like that in their heads, they get a lot more specific about what to do and how to play.

KEY CAPABILITIES

The question to ask your team is what they want their key thrusts or capabilities to be three years from now. In other words, at the end of three years, we will be 'high-fiving' each other because we've developed what capabilities?

Write down the five capabilities you will need in order to be a player in the sandbox described above and to meet the critical numbers you've already determined. For example, at Subserveo, our sandbox was to be the leading North American provider of post-trade compliance solutions for brokerages. The wording became more specific over the years, but that's what it was when we started out. To support that, we determined that our key capabilities would need to be (a) highly available data centers in Canada and the United States, (b) many brokerages using one platform (which would be ours), (c) a self-serving customer platform, which would be (d) mapped to the six, prime, North American data providers, and (e) a fully operational sales and support platform for North American resellers.

When we first listed those capabilities on our OPP, we weren't even close. In fact, we had two customers at the time.

These capabilities map directly from your key differentiating activities in the section that was completed in the Seven Strata of Strategy. We discussed this in the previous chapter. Write them down in the section below the sandbox named Key Thrusts & Capabilities. We've already worked on our brand promise in our Seven Strata of Strategy worksheet, so we're just going to write that down here. As always, continuously confirm it with your team. If the brand promise is new to your organization, it could take a few iterations over time to evolve into what matters most to your customers and differentiates you from your competitors.

Then I ask how we're going to make it hurt if we don't keep our promise (again, from our Seven Strata worksheet), whether that means giving money back to a customer or allowing customers to cancel a contract if they're not happy. If someone expresses reservations about the penalties, then we have a discussion.

The reason I confirm these things over and over again goes back to what I'm committed to as my Key Actions. My fifth action was to over-communicate clarity. This is part of the methodology we came up with in both my companies to keep the rhythm going and continually make sure that our messaging was consistent and clear. I do my quarterly meetings in person or through a videoconference as much as possible so I can see my team's body language when we go through these things and get a sense of whether they truly believe or don't believe. You've got to get to a point where everyone believes.

SWOT ANALYSIS

Before moving to column 4—Goals (1 Yr.)—it is important to make sure you and your team do a reality check on your strengths (internal), weaknesses (internal), opportunities (external), and threats (external). All team members would come prepared because they would already have done their own SWOT analyses with their own teams. Once again, we're trying to unlock the collaborative brain of our whole team. You may recall that we skipped the SWOT analysis on our Business Model Canvas. I like to use a simple process to provoke a good discussion with the team.

Every quarter and at every annual planning session, the team would come prepared to discuss our strengths, weaknesses, opportunities, and threats. We would update the list and then pull out the top three. I would then get everyone to agree that these were our biggest strengths.

Then I'd do the same thing for our weaknesses. Again, we'd write them down and agree on the top three. Strengths and weaknesses are internal, so I do not recommend writing them down in an OPP.

I really don't like to put these things in everyone's face, especially if they are focused in one area. But even if they don't appear here, it's still worth talking them through with the team.

Opportunities and threats are external, so do write them down on your OPP. Next, I'd ask, 'What are our opportunities?' We'd write down what everyone had come up with and agree on the top three. Then we'd do the same for threats. Finally, we'd write the top three opportunities and threats on our plan as a reminder. It is important to socialize the opportunities and threats with the team and board. This is a great way to manage expectations of why the team will deliver or over deliver if these opportunities come to be real, or if a threat could prevent us from delivering on our plan. This is a great discussion to have before the quarter even starts.

COLUMN 4: GOALS (1 YR.)

Next, we move to the one-year view, the company's annual plan. Starting at the top of this column, we need to fill in the financial critical numbers. While building the plan, we would agree on what we were going to track and give a number range. When we had finished building the plan, as mentioned above, we would create the thirty-six-month forecast to support the plan. When this was complete, we would enter the specific twelve-month forecast numbers for what we agreed to track in this column.

Verne Harnish suggests numbers to include here. My team would usually exclude the market cap and focus on economic perfor-mance. We included revenue, expenses, and profit. We wrote down how much cash we wanted to have on hand on 31 December of the next year, because I believe strongly, whether you're profitable or not, everybody needs to know about the cash of the company. We'd have a number for inventory or, in our case, subscriptions. We also tracked revenue per employee and profit per employee.

Column 4 is focused on the annual plan. So, now it's time to work with your team to create the top initiatives for the next twelve months in priority order. We approach this as a team to brainstorm the number-one thing we must accomplish this year in order to be in a good position to reach our three-year targets and plan laid out in column 3. I have done this in many ways, working with my team or with my clients. One effective way to accomplish this is to give all the team members a sticky note to write down the number-one thing they believe should be accomplished for the year. These are all stuck on the wall. Get one of your team members to start grouping the 'stickies' that are similar. Usually, the area with the most 'stickies' becomes the priority to accomplish—but not always. From there you have other areas of focus and can usually work with your team to come up with priorities numbers two to five.

With each of the initiatives created, we are very specific about what will be accomplished by providing a specific date or a deliverable or a measure. We are also specific about who owns each annual initiative. Put their initials beside the initiative in the table. There can only be one person accountable for each initiative.

If we can't come up with the exact metric for measuring our number-one priority—and sometimes you can't—we will not walk away from the meeting without someone owning that initiative. That person will then work with other team members to come up with a plan to deliver our priority and the metrics we can use to ensure we're on track to achieve it within twelve months.

After that come any additional or supporting priorities. You don't have to have five. In my experience, fewer are better.

LEVERAGING ACCOUNTABILITY IN THE ONE PAGE PLAN

Once you set your priorities, it's important to look at who is accountable for them. If a team has five priorities and the same person owns three of them, that's a problem. If that person has to make a decision about where to spend her time, she's going to focus on the number-one priority. That will take precedent over everything else. That means the other two initiatives risk not getting done.

When I look at my 2008 OPP, there were only four people in the company at that point, so my head of sales owned two priorities, my head of operations owned two, and I owned one and the whole OPP. Some people had to own more than one priority because our team was so small, but this should not be the case for a larger company. The ideal situation is to have different members of your executive team own one priority. Whatever your current situation, my fundamental belief is that a priority is not a priority unless it's clear who is responsible for delivering it.

One of the reasons I love an OPP is because, as I mentioned before, one my biggest weakness as a leader, early on, was accountability. That's why I'm adamant about writing down right on this page the initials of the person who owns each priority. It gives people a sense of ownership and pride in delivering. In my companies, we also shared status updates with everyone through my weekly emails. If Joe Bloggs owned the number-one priority, for example, then Joe emailed me every Friday morning to update me on whether the initiative was red (going to miss the target), yellow (offtrack—possibility of missing the target), or green (will make the target). I'd take those updates and send them out to the whole organization, along with my own top note. And every month, Joe Bloggs would get up in front of the group and report on whether we were on track with our number-one priority. Those tactics led to plenty of peer accountability.

The Critical Number section at the bottom of the fourth column has two sections. This section evolved over time in Verne Harnish's OPP, whereby the idea is to find balancing critical numbers. We tried this but always went back to looking for just one critical number. We tried to find a critical number that mattered, that all the teams in the organization could relate to. I have been told this is idealistic but have been successful many times in finding the one number to get the team focused on. The critical number proved to be very important to track as my teams made daily decisions based on our plan. This daily critical number kept us focused on what mattered in our plan and if we were on, ahead, or behind plan, we made the necessary adjustments.

At Paradata, our critical number was the number of new merchants. That affected everybody from IT to support to implementation to sales, and so on. I usually encourage leaders to try their best to narrow this down to just one thing they can measure. It can be really hard to do this, but it's worth working at it until you get there.

If you can't fill out your critical number just yet, think about what it might be and write it down. Brainstorm with your team. It doesn't have to be right, but start with something. Remember, we're always evolving these tools, so whatever you've got is good enough for now. We'll revisit this number later and refine it.

COLUMN 5: ACTIONS (QUARTER)

Column 5 represents the ninety-day plan for the company. This ninety-day plan is in direct relation to column 4—your annual plan. This column represents what you need to accomplish in the next ninety days in order to ensure you stay on track to achieve the annual plan.

The top section of column 5 is a table that represents your financial critical numbers for the quarter. We used the same table as we did for the annual numbers, except this one shows the numbers for the quarter—the next ninety days.

The next section includes the top priorities for the company for the next ninety days. What is it we must get done to move the company closer to its annual goal? I ask the team, 'What is the number-one thing we have to complete within the next ninety days?' That usually leads to a lively discussion to come up with, and agree on, the number-one thing. (If stuck, we use the 'sticky' approach described above.)

We'll come up with who owns that priority and a deliverable date if we can. If we can't, the person who owns it will, after the meeting, get a team together to figure that out and then confirm with the leadership team. And then we'll come up with any other priorities and assign accountability for each.

Our one critical number for the quarter would be based on our annual critical number. If your annual critical number is 1,000 new users, for example, then the quarterly number might be 250, or whatever is necessary to build up the number of new users to 1,000 over four quarters. Just as before, if you can't write that number down, write down what the critical number could be.

COLUMN 7

We are going to skip over to column 6. Once we had columns 1 to 5 filled in after the quarterly meeting, my direct reports would work with their teams or cross-functional teams to create specific plans on the corporate ninety-day initiatives they owned. From there, direct reports would fill out column 7 for themselves. They would fill in their KPIs, the metrics they owned and were accountable for. Then they would fill in the top initiatives that they were accountable for over the next ninety days. These initiatives roll directly up and into the ninety-day corporate initiatives.

Most companies have difficulty working through this part and often ask what happens to their other priorities. I usually ask them what priorities they are talking about, because we just spent four hours to a day coming up with what the leadership team thought was most important to the company. What other priorities are there? This happens mostly with a team that has only been through this quarterly planning process once or twice. They feel that they had a list of priorities and now the corporate priorities are competing with this list. These lists need to be unified. The leadership team just agreed the ninety-day plan contained the most important priorities. Make sure your team leaders' priorities align by getting them to present to the leadership team their individual priorities for the quarter.

COLUMN 5: NINETY-DAY PLAN FOR THE COMPANY

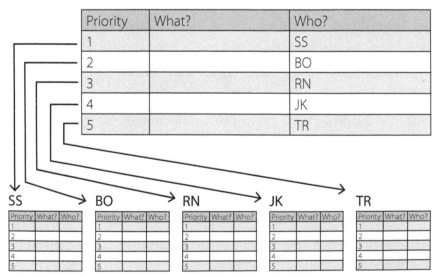

Priority	What?	Who?
1		SS
2		BO
3		RN
4		JK
5		TR

SS → BO → RN → JK → TR

Priority	What?	Who?
1		
2		
3		
4		
5		

These are the individual column 7s per leader in relation to the company 90-day plan.

The last section of column 7 is a critical number for the individual. We did not use this section because we made sure all team leaders had KPIs that matter to delivery of the company's critical numbers. If we did use this section, these individual critical numbers were directly related to the company's critical number.

COLUMN 6: THEME

Column 6 is about creating a theme for your ninety-day plan. I recommend this column gets filled in last. And if you are new to this framework, I usually suggest this column gets filled in after you've worked for three quarters with this methodology.

This column is about creating a theme to get your whole team focused on what needs to be delivered in the next ninety days. This is a way to have fun with your team while keeping them focused on what matters. It gives the team a chance to understand what needs to be delivered in the thirteen-week race, as Verne Harnish calls it, and what will be the reward if the critical number of the quarter is accomplished. It is a great way to increase the teamwork and spirit of the team.

This was always one of my favourite things when I was a team leader. We would come up with an overall theme for the year and then break it down into quarters. We didn't kill ourselves on this, but we didn't assign it to a marketing team either. I wanted the management team to have some fun and get behind it. It just had to be something that resonated with everyone. And then we'd get other teams, especially as we grew bigger, to help us design a scoreboard and come up with ideas for how we were going to celebrate when we met our goals.

One of the themes we came up with was about keeping the 'bus' on the road and making sure that we got from point A to point

B. We called it 'between the ditches', because we were focused on keeping our "bus" on the road and avoiding ditches, crashes, and running out of gas (cash). We had a lot of fun designing a scoreboard, which was a bus that had to bypass a lot of obstacles. We kept moving the bus up the road as we made progress in the number of merchants we added to our platform. And we updated our scoreboard every day. I updated it myself in the beginning, counting up the numbers every night, manually, and sending out an email each morning. The theme kept us focused on our target, and then we knew exactly how we were going to celebrate at the end of the quarter and year when we were successful.

USING YOUR PLAN

I know a lot of CEOs who have filled out an OPP, but when you ask them if they use it regularly and update it every quarter, not many say yes. And if you ask who uses it every month, even fewer say yes. Every week? Every day? Almost no one. But the whole idea is that once you have a handle on the OPP, it should hold you accountable. I print mine out and carry it with me in my notebook. I have an entire war room in my notebook, all the tools we've worked on up to this point. There may be ten pieces of paper, and I have them with me everywhere I go. I also have them on my computer. I can access them on my iPad or my phone. They're up in my office and they're in my home office. I have them everywhere because I use them. They keep me focused on what we need to do.

Once you have this OPP, you can also use it to set your rhythm. This is what the next chapter will explain in detail.

SETTING THE BEAT

Every quarter and at annual meetings confirm with your team what's in your OPP. Go to the Gazelles website (www.gazelles.com) and download a One Page Plan Template.

ACTION ITEMS

1. Go column by column through your OPP, using all the tools you've created up to this point. Fill in as many sections as you can. "Gut it out." Write something down to start or refine if you have been using the OPP for sometime.

2. Do this with your team, confirming as you go that you have consensus on each section.

CHAPTER 8

MEETING BY MEETING

Death by meeting is not what this chapter is about. The key to ensure your culture, strategy, human system, and execution is not looked at only once a year is to plan a year in advance. That way, you'll keep the metronome moving. This means making sure you constantly stay focused on your strategy and execution. Most organizations do not keep this in a regular balance and rhythm.

Below is a chart that shows the rhythm that I developed with my team over many years. We have used a rhythm like this since the year 2000. It comprises meetings and communication tactics to drive the best human behaviour. This is not about meetings for the sake of meetings. This metric rhythm is about leveraging human behaviour and accountability.

Timing	Purpose/Type	Who	How long?
Daily	Connect Meeting	Mgmt. team	15 min. or less
Weekly	Tactical meeting	Mgmt. team	1 hour or less
Weekly	Email	CEO	1 page
Monthly	Confirm strategy/90-day execution plan	Mgmt. team	2 hours or less
Monthly	All-hands meeting	Entire company	1 hour or less
Quarterly	Confirm strategy/plan execution 90 days	Mgmt. team	4 hours or less
Annual	Strategy planning meeting	Mgmt. team	2 days offsite

DAILY MEETING

The daily meeting connects you with your team on a daily basis. This meeting is no longer than fifteen minutes. My leadership team would meet Tuesdays to Fridays, as our weekly meeting was on Mondays, which I will talk more about below. This meeting was a way for us to share good news, share progress to stay focused, and, most importantly, share where we were stuck. If your leadership team members are all in one office, have this meeting standing up. If your team members are not all in one place, use a conference bridge that is always 'open'. The CEO does not have to be the meeting leader all the time. The way we made this meeting most efficient was to have a 'standing agenda'. This means we had the same agenda for every meeting, which drove attendees to come prepared for the agenda items and made the meeting very streamlined.

Our leaders were in two huddles daily: one with their leadership team and one with their own team. In best practice, you have your entire company huddle for forty-five minutes. As an alternative to having many huddles, some companies hold just one full-team huddle daily. The company 1-800-Got-Junk is famous for its whole-team daily huddle. We used this format when we were a start-up, but as we continued to grow, we separated our huddles per team. There is no right or wrong way. Just find a daily meeting that works for your team. Once you start, do not change this meeting for at least thirty days. Be disciplined. Let this habit form.

Daily	Daily Huddle	Mgmt. Team	15 min. or less
Prep	Agenda	Post	
• Good News • Metrics • One thing • Stuck?	• Good news • Metrics • One thing to accomplish in the next 24 hours • Stuck	• Team Leaders have their own huddles.	
Tips and Benefits			
• Build strong relationships. • Use good news to recognize core values. • Reduce the time to connect or respond to email later in the day. • Stay on 'same page'.			

WEEKLY MEETING

The weekly meeting happens once per week. We held all our weekly meetings on Monday mornings, as most of us would be traveling during the week. This was a good way to get everyone in the same room, face to face, before the week really heated up. This meeting was sixty minutes or less. The standing agenda for this meeting is below. Each leadership team member came prepared to discuss these agenda items. You will notice we did not have any time allotted for status updates. This is due to the fact that on the business day before the meeting we all received the current status via email of our ninety-day company priorities and were prepared to discuss the items that were highlighted yellow or red. We would take the first fifteen minutes of the meeting for a quick round robin through the good news, metrics, top priorities, and feedback, and we spent the remainder of the meeting, approximately forty-five minutes, discussing the most important issues related to our plan.

Weekly	Tactical Meeting	Mgmt. Team	1 hour or less
Prep	Agenda	Post	
• Good News • Metrics • Top 3 • Feedback • Prepare items that need to be discussed.	• Good news • Metrics • Top 3 • Feedback • Dynamic	• Team Leaders have their own weekly meeting with their team.	
Tips and Benefits			
• Status is not discussed as the weekly status was received before the meeting. • Use good news to recognize core values. • Feedback: customers, team members, etc. • Dynamic: make a list of the items that need to be discussed; address the items that line up with priorities in the plan.			

WEEKLY MEETING AGENDA BROKEN DOWN

WEEKLY MEETING (60 MIN. OR LESS) MODERATION

Part 1 - Round Robin 12 Min	Part 2 - Feedback 3 - 7 Min	Part 3 - Dynamic Rest of Meeting
• Good News • Metrics • Top 3	• Team member feedback • Customer feedback • Market feedback • All feedback	• Make list of all that needs to be discussed. • Leader decides, based on priorities.

WEEKLY EMAIL

The weekly email is just that. As CEO, I would send out this email every Friday afternoon at the earliest, and Sunday evening at the latest, to announce where we were in our quarterly plan. This email was 'rolled up' from the whole company, literally.

Weekly Email	Email	CEO	1 Page
Prep	Email Structure	Post	
• All team members report to their team leader status of their priorities each week.	• Good news • Metrics • Priority status • Close on positive note	• Prep. for discussion of yellows and red in your weekly meeting.	
Tips and Benefits			
• Use good news to recognize core values. • Each team member should take no longer than 5 minutes to create status update.			

The idea behind this weekly email was not the email itself, but the action of getting team members to look at their quarterly priorities and inform their team leaders of their status. Having all team members look at their initiatives as least once weekly was a way to make sure we all stayed focused on what mattered to the delivery of the plan.

Every Thursday, starting at noon, team members would email the status of their priorities to their team leader. This status update would take no longer than five minutes. The team leaders would create their status update from what was received and send their update to their team leader, and so on, until I received the status from my direct reports, who owned the top priorities of the company for the quarter. By noon on Friday I would have created a table with red, green, and yellow for each of the company's top five priorities for the ninety-day plan. I would then add good news, critical number metrics, and the priorities update before closing the email on a very positive note and letting people know where I was going to be that week. So simple but so effective.

WEEKLY EMAIL SENT FROM CEO

Send to Whole Team →

To...	Ateam@greatcompany.com
Subject	Please Read - Weekly Round Up

Hello All,

Start with Good News →

Good News

- Great week at the tradeshow in Orlando—150 leads—marketing team did an excellent job presenting our organization. Great work!!
- John Smith—from our call center—headed off a major issue with one of our largest customers. Thanks, John, for your quick collaborative approach.

Share Critical Number →

Metrics

	Week	Month	Quarter	Year to Date
New Users	50/50	50/200	50/600	50/2400

Share Status →

Quality Priorities

Priority	What	Who	Status	Comments
1		SS	GREEN	
2		BO	YELLOW	Organized meeting for Monday to discuss with team.
3		RN	RED	We underestimated time for build. We need to adjust time or requirements. Meeting set for Monday first thing.
4		JK	GREEN	
5		TR	GREEN	

Close Strong and Positive →

[Close Off: use a positive closing and let people know where you will be that week.]

Thank you.

Lots of companies use dashboards, dashboard software. I did not use these tools because they so often get overlooked. This indirect weekly action of emailing team members ensured we were getting our ninety-day plan completed.

MONTHLY MEETING

Monthly	Confirm Strategy/90-day Execution Plan	Mgmt. Team	2 hours or less
Prep	Agenda	Post	
• Good News • Metrics • Top 3 • Feedback • Prepare items that need to be discussed.	• Good news • Metrics • Confirm qtrly. plan • Top 3 for month • Feedback • Dynamic	• Team Leaders have their own monthly meeting with their team.	
Tips and Benefits			
• Use good news to recognize core values. • Feedback: customers, team members, etc. • Dynamic: make a list of the items that need to be discussed; address the items that line up with priorities in the plan.			

The monthly meeting in our rhythm took place on the fourth Monday of every month instead of our weekly meeting. The purpose of this meeting was to confirm we still believed our strategy to be true and to ensure we were on track for our ninety-day plan. This meeting was no longer than two hours. A lot of CEOs I have worked with usually do not have a monthly meeting. It is critical for a leadership team to have a face-to-face meeting during the quarter. I have had very positive feedback on these meetings from the team leaders and

CEOs. I, myself, found this to be a critical two-hour check in. Team leaders would have their own team monthly meeting as well.

MONTHLY 'ALL-HANDS' MEETING

Monthly	All-Hands Meeting	Entire Company	1 hour or less
Prep	Agenda	Post	
• Good News • Metrics • Confirm qtrly. plan • Status qtrly. plan • Team core value recognition	• Good news • Metrics • Confirm qtrly. plan • Status qtrly. plan • Q&A • Team core value recognition	• Team building/gathering supporting 13-week race on theme.	
Tips and Benefits			
• Use good news to recognize core values. • Get whole team together. • Everyone gets direct interaction with leadership and in-person chance to set tone for the month.			

This meeting was scheduled in the last week of every month. We never missed this meeting, no matter what was happening. The whole team would be in attendance at this meeting. We did a round robin of good news from the whole team. We would review our critical numbers and confirm the status of our quarterly plan. The whole leadership team would be involved with this. There was a very lively question and answer period. We acknowledged and recognized team members who were 'oozing' the core values. This meeting was my chance to set the tone for the month and to get to hear from all. We had a very transparent culture so there was no holding back in the

Q&A session. This always gave me a good feel for where the team heads were.

QUARTERLY MEETING

Quarterly	Confirm Strategy/Plan Execution 90 Days	Mgmt. Team	4 hours or less
Prep	Agenda	Post	
• Map • Forces • CC flow chart • SWOT • Team-created priorities • A player review • Functional rev. • Metrics • Feedback	• Good news • Metrics • Status qtrly. plan • Core ideologies • Functional rev. • CC flow chart • Strategic analysis • Confirm strategy • SWOT • Qtrly. initiatives • Critical numbers • One phase close	• Meet with team to confirm plan. • Confirm deliverables. • Get buy-in. • Meet with leadership for one hour to confirm qtrly. plans.	
Tips and Benefits			
• Use good news to recognize core values. • Team leaders meet with team BEFORE qtrly. meeting. • Team leaders meet with team AFTER qtrly. meeting. • Leadership team confirms qtrly. plan before qtr. starts.			

This quarterly meeting, as shown above, gets the whole company involved in the strategic and execution planning. To prepare for this meeting, the team leaders take the time to meet with their teams to gather feedback on the company SWOT, company priorities, and other feedback. This is a way to get the whole team to buy in to the quarterly plan by starting with the team. Following all the team leaders' team meetings, we would then have the quarterly meeting with my direct reports.

QUARTERLY MEETING (4 HRS. OR LESS) AGENDA

Part 1 - Round Robin - 5 Min
• Good News • Metrics
Part 2 - Status Current Qtrly Plan - 5–10 Min
• Reality check on current qtrly. plan
Part 3 - Strategic Analysis
• Core ideologies - confirm • Functional Review • CC flow chart analysis • Strategic analysis • Confirm strategy
Part 4 - Qtrly. Plan
• SWOT • Qtrly. initiatives • Critical numbers
Part 5 - Close Round Robin
• One-phrase close

We would start with good news and metrics and then make sure we were clear on our quarterly status. This meeting took place in the third week of the third month of the quarter. We confirmed columns 1 and 2 of the plan, core ideologies, and we worked a team cohesive exercise from Pat Lencioni's *Five Dysfunctions of a Team*. We would also confirm our Function Accountability Chart (FACe), focusing on clarity of role and leading and lagging indicators.

STRATEGIC ANALYSIS - APPROACH

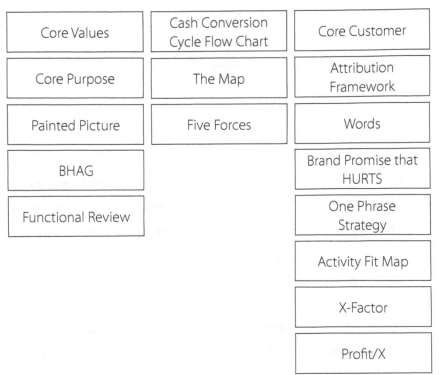

Core Values	Cash Conversion Cycle Flow Chart	Core Customer
Core Purpose	The Map	Attribution Framework
Painted Picture	Five Forces	Words
BHAG		Brand Promise that HURTS
Functional Review		One Phrase Strategy
		Activity Fit Map
		X-Factor
		Profit/X

After that, we would discuss the deltas of the cash conversion flow chart, The Map, Porter's Five Forces, the Activity Map, the Business Model Canvas, and the Seven Strata. The key to accomplishing all this is that (a) all of these tools must be visual, and (b) all team leaders must have prepped to discuss deltas. This ensures a thorough but speedy review. The more the CEO makes this a habit and stays disciplined with the agenda, the more likely this will happen easily, quarter over quarter. This strategic analysis is critical to ensure your strategy and execution aligns both internally and externally.

WAR ROOM - ON THE WALL

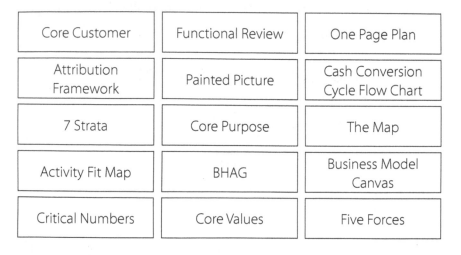

Core Customer	Functional Review	One Page Plan
Attribution Framework	Painted Picture	Cash Conversion Cycle Flow Chart
7 Strata	Core Purpose	The Map
Activity Fit Map	BHAG	Business Model Canvas
Critical Numbers	Core Values	Five Forces

The next step in the meeting is to conduct a reality check by looking at the SWOT analysis completed in the previous quarter and seeing what has changed. The team leaders come prepared for this discussion. From there, you must come up with the number-one thing that must be accomplished in the next ninety days. Then you must brainstorm the other priorities. One of the tactics I use to make sure the whole leadership team weighs in is 'stickies'. Get them to write down on a sticky note all the initiatives and then group them and discuss them. This is a quick way to get to the heart of the discussion. The financial critical numbers are pulled from the financial forecast and annual plan that was created at the beginning of the year and validated.

Don't be worried if you cannot keep the quarterly meeting to four hours or less. The most important part is to make sure you have a quarterly meeting. Most of my clients today are taking a full day to ensure they are covering all that is needed as they implement this methodology. Some companies are taking up to two days.

QUARTERLY MEETING DANCE – 3RD MONTH IN QTR.

M	T	W	Th	F
		Prep: team leaders meet with their team		
		Leadership qtrly. meeting	Confirm: team leaders meet with their team	
		Confirm: leadership qtrly. plan		

A key point is that, following the quarterly meeting, each team leader should already have a follow-up team meeting booked to discuss the quarterly plan and the priorities that the team leader owns and, in turn, the team owns. The team leaders will confirm the corporate priorities that they own with dates, metrics, and deliverables. There will be one more meeting in the last week of the third month of the quarter for the leadership to make the quarterly plan final. This should be completed before the start of the quarter.

One of the important behavioural changes this process leverages is that the whole team is involved in the planning process. When the actual OPP is presented for the quarter, no one is surprised by what's in the plan and, most importantly, the team feels huge ownership because they are involved in creating the plan. This is fundamental.

I recently moderated one of the quarterly meetings of one of my clients. At the last planning meeting, the company only involved the top executives. I had an opportunity to meet with the operational leaders and get their feedback on the plan, and it was what I had expected: this plan was owned by the executive team. It was not the operational leaders' plan. At the quarterly planning meeting I moderated, all leaders together, for the first time, created the next quarterly plan. What a difference. The team walked out with full ownership of the plan and their execution focus is now at a different level, due to the fact they were involved in creating the plan. This is very human and expected behaviour.

ANNUAL PLANNING MEETING

Annual	Strategy Planning Meeting	Mgmt. Team	2 days offsite
Prep	Agenda	Post	
• Map • Forces • CC flow chart • SWOT • Team created priorities • A player review • Functional rev. • Metrics • Feedback	• Good news • Metrics • Status qtrly. plan • Core ideologies • Functional rev. • CC flow chart • Strategic analysis • Confirm strategy • SWOT • Qtrly. initiatives • Critical numbers • One-phrase close	• Meet with team to confirm plan. • Confirm deliverables. • Get buy-in. • Meet with leadership for one hour to confirm annual plans. • Create thirty six month forecast. • Approval from board.	
Tips and Benefits			
• Use good news to recognize core values. • Team leaders meet with team BEFORE meeting. • Team leaders meet with team AFTER meeting. • Leadership team confirms plan before year starts.			

All companies I work with have an annual planning meeting over two days. Some are held offsite and some are not. The key is to renew the team, take a detailed deep dive into the strategic analysis, and create an annual plan. Again, the team leaders need to take the time to prepare for the meeting with their teams and, after the meeting, confirm the plan with their teams and adjust as required. Following this meeting, the financial forecast is created for the next thirty-six months, month over month. The meeting is held in the second month of the fourth quarter to allow enough time to get the plan finalized before the end of the year.

I have worked at companies that, because of their size, started this process in the third quarter. The important part of this planning was that we created an annual plan first and then worked through the financial forecast to support it—not the other way around.

The one agenda item that appears at the end of the standing agenda for the quarterly and annual meetings is the one-phrase close. This is the last thing you do before closing out the meeting. In a round robin, the attendees 'gut out' a one-phrase close on how they feel at that moment. You will get answers like 'overwhelmed', 'excited', 'let's do it', 'cautiously optimistic', and so on. This provides the leader with good information as to who is fired up and whom the leader might need to work with to ensure their comfort with the direction and plan. For me, personally, this is critical feedback on which to build with teams and clients.

One of the other standing rules we had in place with our team was the 80 percent rule. Meaning when agreeing on the plan if you are 80 percent of the way in agreement you must walk out of the room 100 percent in agreement. If team members are not 80 percent of the way to an agreement, you must convince them to change the plan, or the team must convince you to be at least 80 percent in agreement. This was a way to ensure that people who were not in agreement spoke up, and in some cases, based that feedback, we needed to drastically change our plan. As the leader, you must make sure the whole team walks out of this meeting 100 percent aligned with the plan, and this is a great way to get that alignment.

Rhythm Key	
Daily	D
Weekly	W
Weekly Email	WE
Monthly	M
All-Hands	TH
Quarterly	Qtr.
Annual	A
Board Meeting	BM

Create your metronome effect through the planned rhythms in your organization. The above Rhythm Key shows the meetings we decided to have in our companies. This is what worked for us. If you do not have an idea of what works, you can use this as a default and adjust from there.

Once you decide on the meetings, take a calendar for the year and overlay all the different types of meetings. This sounds quite meticulous, but as the leader you can easily see what is going to happen, and your team members can schedule their preparation meetings supporting this rhythm. This approach ensures you do not miss a meeting because you did not find time to schedule it.

I was recently asked in a workshop if I start by sharing this view with the team. It is an excellent question. If you are, for the first time, setting this rhythm up in your company, I recommend that you plan the rhythm yourself and then set the meetings up in your calendar by inviting the team to the meetings. This will get these meetings into the calendar without overwhelming your team. When team members schedule for the year, they wonder when they are going to get their 'real' work done. Once this rhythm is in place, I work with the team to adjust the rhythm as required to make it most effective. Below is a high-level view of the rhythm that was described above.

Q1-Month 1

M	T	W	Th	F
W	D	D	D	D WE
W	D	D	D	D WE
W	D	D BM	D	D WE
M	D	D TH	D	D WE

Q1-Month 2

M	T	W	Th	F
W	D	D	D	D WE
W	D	D	D	D WE
W	D	D	D	D WE
M	D	D TH	D	D WE

Q1-Month 3

M	T	W	Th	F
W	D	D	D	D WE
W	D	D	D	D WE
W	D	D Qtr	D	D WE
M	D	D TH	D	D WE

Q2-Month 1

M	T	W	Th	F
W	D	D	D	D WE
W	D	D	D	D WE
W	D	D BM	D	D WE
M	D	D TH	D	D WE

Q2-Month 2

M	T	W	Th	F
W	D	D	D	D WE
W	D	D	D	D WE
W	D	D	D	D WE
M	D	D TH	D	D WE

Q2-Month 3

M	T	W	Th	F
W	D	D	D	D WE
W	D	D	D	D WE
W	D	D Qtr	D	D WE
M	D	D TH	D	D WE

Q3-Month 1

M	T	W	Th	F
W	D	D	D	D WE
W	D	D	D	D WE
W	D	D BM	D	D WE
M	D	D TH	D	D WE

Q3-Month 2

M	T	W	Th	F
W	D	D	D	D WE
W	D	D	D	D WE
W	D	D	D	D WE
M	D	D TH	D	D WE

Q3-Month 3

M	T	W	Th	F
W	D	D	D	D WE
W	D	D	D	D WE
W	D	D Qtr	D	D WE
M	D	D TH	D	D WE

Q4-Month 1

M	T	W	Th	F
W	D	D	D	D WE
W	D	D	D	D WE
W	D	D BM	D	D WE
M	D	D TH	D	D WE

Q4-Month 2

M	T	W	Th	F
W	D	D	D	D WE
W	D A	D A	D	D WE
W	D	D	D	D WE
M	D	D TH	D	D WE

Q4-Month 3

M	T	W	Th	F
W	D	D	D	D WE
W	D	D	D	D WE
W	D	D Qtr	D	D WE
M	D	D TH	D	D WE

The best practice in setting your rhythm is to book meetings for a year in advance, establish the standing agendas, support your team leaders in their preparation meeting with their team, and make sure you get regular feedback on the rhythm itself.

ACTION ITEMS

1. Create your plan to implement your rhythm by printing out a blank calendar for the year and writing down month over month your meeting and communication rhythm. Book these meetings in your calendar and invite attendees.

2. Create and make known your standing agendas for all meetings and communications.

3. Book and start your daily huddles this week.

4. Support your leadership team with their team meetings to prepare for the leadership meetings.

CHAPTER 9

FORECASTING PROFIT

This chapter is about connecting your One Page Plan (OPP) to your forecasted profit. So many of the strategic plans I've reviewed over the years are not connected to the company's forecast. Sometimes all a company has is a budget, and neither a financial forecast nor a strategic plan has been created. But since we have already completed our strategic analysis and we have an OPP, let's put our money where our mouth is.

For an established company that already has a forecast, the idea is that you want to take the OPP you've just created and line it up with your financial forecast. If you said that a year from now you'll be doing A, B, and C, you have to make sure that those initiatives are reflected in your financial plan. What do you have to invest in to accomplish A? What will your reward be if you accomplish it? You've got to see these things reflected in your financial plan on a very detailed level.

And for those companies that don't have a formal financial forecast, this is the time to create one, using the information and priorities that were written down on the OPP.

REVISITING YOUR CASH CONVERSION FLOW CHART

Before creating a future view of your financials, it's a good idea to take another look at the current state of cash within your organization. We created a cash conversion flow chart in Chapter 2 and looked at the number of days it took to go from a sales lead to collecting cash in hand. What I like to do at this point is to take that flow chart and colour the activities in that chain. If it's an efficient process, colour it in green. If it could use a bit of improvement, colour it in yellow. The glaringly low-hanging fruit should be in red.

Each quarter, you want to work through this and improve on those parts you colored red or yellow. What we're aiming for here is to make everything green. We want the shortest possible timeframe for getting cash into the business so we can use it to grow. And that growth will be reflected in our financial forecast.

BUILDING YOUR FINANCIAL FORECAST

I have used the same basic framework to create forecasts for about twelve years. It includes what I call an assumptions page, as well as formal financials on spreadsheets and worksheets.

I usually start by creating the assumptions page. That page is a list of all the assumptions I can make about profit, revenue, expenses, people, and so on.

Next, create a basic P&L, a pretty detailed one for revenue and expenses. I use that to start filling in the numbers on my OPP, the revenue I expect, based on my plan. Then work on expenses, which should be grouped into sales expenses, marketing expenses, R&D expenses, and operational expenses—whatever your expense categories are—to come up with a template. Underneath those headings, go into more detail.

From there, for each of the sections in my high-level P&L, do a month-over-month. That's really important. Drag out thirty-six months of month-over-months. And then I might say, 'Hey, head of sales, we've got certain things we said we are going to do in our plan. Please come back with revenue spreadsheets that reflect that.' This process works for very large companies and small, alike.

It's so liberating to get help from your team members. You know the head of sales is going to come back after working with the financial team to come up with the numbers. And the finance team will usually create a template for teams to fill out. They'll do one for sales, one for marketing, and one for development for every team leader. As CEO, I have the responsibility to forecast profit. I would start with forecasting the profit and then work with my team to validate this forecast, based on our OPP.

After all the team leaders have made their contributions, we pull it all together into one big plan. When we come together to review and finalize our quarterly or annual OPP, we're going to look at how that plan is tied into our financials. We're going to look at both and approve both at the same time. You may have your CFO and your financial team do the work on this, but when I started both my companies, I drove this process myself.

WHY DO THIS?

I think this discipline is an absolute must. When I've talked to business leaders about creating forecasts, they have sometimes told me how hard they are to do and I have agreed with them. It's hard to create a detailed financial plan month over month for thirty-six months, but I'll tell you, without it, it's really hard to hold yourself or your team accountable for meeting the goals you've spelt out on your OPP. Creating forecasts keeps your plan grounded in financial reality.

Doing this in a detailed way will also help you get your ideal critical number for your OPP. In my companies, there were times when we weren't sure what we were doing, especially the first time we tried to come up with our critical number. There wasn't a book to follow at that point, but we really worked through this, as a team. And once we got our critical number, it remained the same until we sold the company. Even after we sold the company, that number became the critical number of the bigger company that bought us.

As I mentioned before, our critical number at Subserveo was the number of users per day. That critical number drove everything in our plan. The more users we had, the more servers we needed; the more room we needed in our databases, the more IT people we needed to manage those servers; the more support people we needed, the more phone lines we needed; and so on. The number drove everything.

I know it's hard, but I assure you that you can find your critical number if you get into enough detail in your forecast. I'm not going to tell you this is an easy step. It will take some time, and you won't get it right on day one. But that's OK, as long as you're working on it quarter over quarter, month over month. If your company is a small company, you, as CEO, are probably going to be the finance person who takes this on, and there's no better way to learn your business. In bigger companies, the CFO will work on this, and I encourage that person to really go into detail, to really plan out the entire thirty-six months, month over month. I've worked with a lot of companies that only plan out twelve months, and report quarterly, but you need the discipline to extend your forecast over thirty-six months and report on it monthly.

This framework, which I built with my team, is a way to see progress month over month and a way to figure out where adjustments might be needed. The more history you have in your business, the easier it will be to forecast your profit. The other advantage is that it will help you get processes in place so that you can close out your month end as fast as possible. It makes it a quicker process.

We talked a bit in Chapter 2 about coming up with what you want your profit to be and working backwards from there. But you then have to balance that against what your profit is actually going to be. It could be that because you invested in certain things this year, it's going to be a break-even year. It happens. Or maybe it will be a break-even year if you don't adjust some of your key initiatives. Whatever the case, the key thing is that you create your plan together with your team and then look at it alongside your financials. It's a great way to get the whole executive team involved in your financials, not just the CFO and the CEO.

I'm a very transparent person when it comes to numbers. Once we have the numbers, I'll show a summary view of them in monthly 'all-hands' meetings. It's a view people can grasp. It says, 'Here's where we were. Here's what we said we were going to do, and here's what we've done.' It helps people get a fuller picture of where their company is and how far it is from where they want to be.

SETTING THE BEAT

Every quarter and at annual meetings review your financials alongside your OPP.

ACTION ITEMS

1. Revisit your cash conversion flow chart and look for ways to improve so you have more cash on hand for growth.

2. Create a thirty-six-month, month-over-month financial forecast. Start with forecasting your profit. This won't happen overnight, but keep at it and be as detailed as you can be.

3. Line up your OPP with your financial forecast. Make sure the goals and initiatives in your plan are reflected in your forecast. This is about putting your money where your mouth is!

CHAPTER 10

TEAM COHESIVENESS

As a leader, you have to make your team your number-one priority, which means that team cohesiveness is not something you can outsource to HR. If you recall, it was one of the key actions I listed for myself on my One Page Plan (OPP). It must be engrained in the rhythm you, as the CEO or leader, set and make a part of all meetings and interactions, where appropriate. Look back at the graphic at the end of the introduction, and you'll see that team cohesiveness makes up one of the walls of our house. If you take away that wall, the house won't stand. That's how important this piece is. Without it, your house will crumble. It's the leaders' responsibility to make their team cohesive, the wall of their house strong. When I first read Patrick Lencioni's book *The Five Temptations of a CEO*, I used it for my own evaluation. The best next step you can take, as a leader, is to share this information with your team. When I did this, my team became really interested in reading the book and assessing their own biggest temptations. After they did, we all shared our biggest temptations with the group. We continued to do this on a rhythmical basis, of course, within our annual planning sessions, and we kept doing it because it allowed us to be continuously aware of ourselves and of how we functioned as a whole. It greatly improved our relationships and our communications.

When Lencioni came out with *The Five Dysfunctions of a Team*, we used this framework, because it was directly aligned with building a strong, cohesive team. Since ensuring team cohesiveness is one of your most important roles as a leader, you have to build time into your rhythm to work on it. That's the only way to guarantee it will happen. And Lencioni's *Five Dysfunctions of a Team* provides a framework for the CEO or leader to do just that.

To get started, my whole management team read the book. It's a quick and easy read, and I encourage all leaders to get their teams to do the same. We also bought the facilitator's guide, which Lencioni published to accompany the book. Then we went step by step through the process to better understand how we functioned as a team. We asked ourselves if there was an absence of trust, a fear of conflict, a lack of commitment, an avoidance of accountability, or inattention to results. And where we were on Lencioni's pyramid.

You can run through the Five Dysfunctions with your team all at once or you can do it over time. My recommendation is to do it over time as it's a lot to take in all at once. Besides that, every time you add a new person to your team, it's going to create a new dynamic, so you have to go back and start with the very foundation: trust. As a team, we worked this into our monthly meetings, our quarterly meetings, and our annual meetings so it became an established part of our rhythm. As the leader of these sessions, I would use different questions from the *Five Dysfunctions of a Team* facilitator's guide to focus on a specific area of the framework during each meeting, depending on where we were in our growth as a strong, cohesive team.

At minimum, you should spend time confirming your team is cohesive every quarter. Because if you're not cohesive, and you walk out of meetings without being aligned, the rest of the company will see it. If you don't have a cohesive management team, it can block your ability to grow.

I recommend that you work time into every meeting to maintain your team's cohesiveness. This is an evolutionary process, but your focus on it is critical to the team's success.

Patrick Lencioni's Five Dysfunctions of a Team

1. Absence of trust

2. Fear of conflict

3. Lack of commitment

4. Avoidance of accountability

5. Inattention to results

KNOWING AND TRUSTING

You can hire a facilitator to take you through Lencioni's *Five Dysfunctions of a Team*, or you can have someone in your company lead these sessions by using Lencioni's facilitator's guide. I strongly recommend that the CEO does it. I didn't use anyone to facilitate in the early days of learning this process.

When we first went through the Five Dysfunctions program, I probably followed the guide more closely than I do now. We started with a team assessment, as the guide suggests. At the time, there weren't many online tools, but, today, you can find assessment tools on Lencioni's website, which will give you a good feel for where your team is right now: how strong you are in each of the five areas and where you need the most improvement. But regardless of what the assessment reveals, I always start at the beginning with trust.

When talking about trust, I often used some key questions from Lencioni's framework to kick things off. For example, I would ask what position people held in their families, meaning youngest, oldest, or somewhere in between. Then I'd ask where they were born. The third thing I liked to ask was, 'What was the most memorable event of your childhood?' Then we'd go around the room and everyone would answer the questions. It's very hard to trust someone without knowing that person, so that's where we'd start. And the answers you get can be amazing.

I've worked with many of the same people for over ten years now, so I don't always start off by asking about people's position in their families or where they were born. After the first time, I already knew those things. It's important to change things, since you're going to cover these topics again and again. I might ask instead what was the most difficult thing, or the most important thing, or the most unique challenge of their childhood. What's often interesting is that even though you think you know people well, answers can change, depending on what has happened to them within the previous year. Even with people you know, there are always more things to know.

These are more than just icebreakers. The answers to these questions can really help you understand why someone is the way he is. Lencioni's book gives a good example of a CFO who was driving people nuts because he was so tight with money and he couldn't pry his fingers off the castle. But then, the team learned he'd grown up in a poor family in which it was really important to hold on tight to every last penny because they didn't have anything to spare. That kind of information can help you understand where someone is coming from. And if you understand better, you'll approach that person differently.

I'd spent five years with some of my team members before we started working this into our quarterly meetings. And when we did, I was almost embarrassed by what I didn't know about people I'd known for years. In working with other companies, I've found this is a common occurrence when this tactic is introduced.

When I'm brought into another company as a coach, I often ask this kind of question of the team I'm working with. I ask them to share some personal things with me and I participate as well. It's a way of quickly getting to know something about each other and creating trust within the group.

What we're trying to accomplish when we talk about trust is getting people to be vulnerable. Being honest with people about what you think and who you are isn't easy. It can make many people uncomfortable. But the more you talk about these things, the easier it becomes.

HEALTHY CONFLICT

The next step is to try to remove the fear of conflict and create constructive conflict among your team members. A team can't master conflict without trust, so these things really build on one another.

At one point there was someone on my team whom I'd known for five years and who had a different way of dealing with conflict. I would characterize it as avoiding conflict. When we were going through this step, I asked a question from Lencioni's framework about Sunday dinners and what they were like when people were growing up. He answered that when his family ate dinner together (which they didn't do regularly), there was no conflict at the table. In fact, there was never any conflict at any time. His family just didn't argue about things.

This was fascinating to me because my own experience had been just the opposite. My family had dinner together every Sunday and we had no problem expressing our opinions to the point where someone might get mad and leave the table. But then, they'd come back later and we'd all just carry on.

When I thought about the differences in our stories, I realized I was going to have to work with this individual a bit differently to help him get comfortable with conflict. After all, he was part of the team that was going to decide on a direction for the entire company, and I wanted us all to walk in unison. We were going to have to encourage him to voice his opinions, even his disagreement, if they ever arose.

What I like to do in terms of conflict is understand where everybody is coming from and establish how we're going to get through conflict, as a team. One of my favourite tactics is to divide the group into teams. If we were trying to decide on a particular item and, say, four people on the team agreed and three people didn't, it was up to the four people who agreed to convince the others to see it their way. Or it could be the other way around. Banding together in groups was a really positive way to get disagreement out on the table.

As described in the last chapter, we used the 80 percent rule. For those who were uncomfortable with conflict, the meeting leader would go around the room and ask each person directly, 'Are you on board?' Someone who was hesitant to speak up might then say, 'No, I'm not' and explain why. If you hadn't asked directly, you might have left the meeting, thinking everyone was in agreement.

We set up those rules very early on, which helped us get to the point where we could always find a way to get on the same page through positive conflict.

HOW DO YOU KNOW?

There are a number of ways you can tell if your team is not cohesive. First, you have to listen to feedback from the larger team. It's often people outside your direct team who will notice first if you're going in different directions. Another clue is when all the team members look you in the eyes and say, 'Yes, we agree; we got it', but then they go off to execute poorly. The people who didn't agree and didn't say anything might even say something like 'I told you so'.

I'm also big on getting feedback through cross-functional team meetings. I would always have my team leaders put together a multifunctional team of maybe ten people to come and sit down with me when I was visiting various offices. Then, we'd have a straight-up conversation. You can get a lot of information that way through what is said and not said. I would take notes of every question asked and often realize how many things I didn't know the answer to or should have been forthcoming with so the question did not have to be asked. I'd find myself thinking, 'Wow, we're not doing a good job here', or 'Why are they asking something like that?'

Lencioni's team assessment tools can also be really useful to start off with. They might give you some surprising insights.

STAYING COHESIVE

The metronome effect is different from just setting a rhythm to execute. The metronome effect takes into consideration your strategic rhythm, execution rhythm, and your team cohesiveness. You can make sure your team stays cohesive by having a rhythm in place that makes certain you work on your cohesiveness on a regular basis. On an annual basis, my team would have a two-day strategic planning session, and we would talk about the Five Dysfunctions during that time. I would usually take an hour out of the morning and the afternoon sessions, both days, to do this, so we would spend anywhere from four to five hours on this in total. I might even take a half-day before our annual planning if I had a new team, because we're not going to have a good planning session if our team dynamics aren't working well.

Then, in our quarterly meetings, we'd either build on what we did in our annual meeting or, if someone new had joined the team, we'd start back at the beginning, so we could quickly build trust with the new team member. If my team had any big problems with cohesiveness, we'd go back even further and review our core values. Do we all have the same core values? Check. OK, then, why are we not cohesive? Usually, the answer came back to a lack of trust, so we would start from there.

I believe that what we did worked, as we didn't try to create a new rhythm for this particular subject. We just made team cohesiveness part of our already established rhythm, which made me realize what the Metronome Effect methodology meant to the success of our goals. As a leader, you have to have one rhythm and work your strategic tools, your team tools, your cash tools, and your execution tools into that rhythm. That's how people come to expect that this is a part of what an organization does.

WHY IT MATTERS

A team that's cohesive is a team that usually wins, but a team that's not cohesive, even if it has the best players, won't always win. I played on a few sports teams that showed me this. The least skilled team I ever played on had really great leadership and coaching, which led to a collaborative team spirit that took us really far.

The team that I'm speaking of was the Nova Scotia field hockey team I played on when I was sixteen. We competed in the Canada Summer Games, which are the country's U21 games, where the best players compete from every province. I had played soccer since I was five, but I was new to field hockey. Still, I was encouraged to try out for the Nova Scotia team and made it. The coaches chose people based on athleticism and attitude over skill. They had some core values they believed in and were looking for in team members, but they figured they could teach us the skills we didn't have.

Nova Scotia's field hockey team had never gone to a finals or won a medal in the Canada Games. Nonetheless, our team goal was to win the gold medal. That's a pretty lofty goal for a team that could only play together outdoors for two or three months out of the year, especially when competing with teams from Central and Western Canada that practiced all year long. Some of the provinces, like British Columbia and Ontario, were also highly funded. Those had the powerhouse teams.

My team had a mental coach, a physical coach, and a skills coach. There was no one on the team who, from a skill level, was a star. Instead, what our coaches stressed was how we were going to play together as a team. We did team-building exercises together on and off the field, and I've used a number of them since in my companies.

I remember being asked to sit in a circle after practice. We didn't know what we were going to do at first, but then the coach asked us to say one thing we liked about the person sitting next to us and one thing we didn't like or something that person needed to improve. We went around the circle that way. I've done that with many teams since, and it really brings the team members closer together and makes them self-aware.

We made it to the finals that year and then lost the gold-medal game 1-0. We were really disappointed. But if you think about it, no one ever thought we'd ever make it that far. For me, looking back, the silver medal was great, but the real win was understanding how to build a cohesive team that could strive for a big goal.

A lot of people ask me, 'You have three degrees. How does the academic world apply to your entrepreneurial world, to building companies?' I reply, 'Well, you have to know how to set goals and learn the material things to get there, and my education was excellent for that. But the best experiences I took away from university were from the different varsity teams I played on.'

I played basketball and field hockey, and I ran track. We had international players on our varsity teams as well as players from different parts of Canada and the United States. They came from all kinds of ethnic and income backgrounds, and we had to figure out how to play together as a team. One of my teams, which I was captain of, was having a few problems with some of our young stars who had come from other countries, so we had to become creative about how we were going to work together. One of our coach's rules was that if someone was late for practice, everyone else had to run until that player showed up. And if they didn't show up, the rest of us would run for the whole two hours. After doing that a few times, the team made darn sure everyone showed up on a time. We figured out the team members who weren't very punctual or did not care if they were late. We arranged for a team member to meet those players after class and hustle them to practice.

Everything I learned back then about core values, why a team exists, what's expected of a team member, and the rhythm of a team all applies to business. I once had the opportunity to listen to Pat Riley, the former head coach of the Miami Heat, talk about how he pulled that team together and made them successful. He was speaking at a business conference. They closed out the same business conference with Andre Agassi. The things I learned from sports about how to create a cohesive team have been invaluable in building companies.

SETTING THE BEAT

Work on team cohesiveness at least **every quarter.** When a new team member joins your team, start at the very beginning with Trust.

ACTION ITEMS

1. Make team cohesiveness your number-one priority. Start by reading *The Five Temptations of a CEO* by Patrick Lencioni, and share your biggest temptation with your team. Get your team to read it, too, and share their biggest temptation.

2. Read the *Five Dysfunctions of a Team* by Patrick Lencioni, or attend a facilitated workshop to jump-start your understanding.

3. Use Lencioni's online tools or facilitator's guide to assess your team's cohesiveness in each of the five areas.

4. Work through all Five Dysfunctions with your team on a continual basis to stay on track. Start from the beginning with trust every time someone new joins the team. Make this a part of your Metronome Effect methodology, starting today.

CHaPTeR 11

HUMAN SYSTEM

If your team is your number-one priority, as we talked about in the last chapter, your human system has to be the number-one process that you, as the leader, make sure is in place within your organization. The consistent processes that make up your human system will ensure that the right team members are in the right roles with the right skills, growing and loving it!

This is about putting processes in place to make sure your team members will be successful. Your human system starts at the very beginning with the foundation of the core values of the company. It starts when you first begin an interview process with a candidate, and it continues throughout that person's time with your organization, providing you with a way to regularly assess her value and hold her accountable.

The human system that we created was based on our Core Ideologies and Topgrading. I was fortunate enough to be able to bring my team to a Topgrading workshop led by Brad Smart, the author of the book *Topgrading*, at an ACETECH event in Vancouver, British Columbia. I really got behind their work because we were able to take the Topgrading system they suggested and work it into our already established rhythm. That system also ensured that, nine times out of ten, we hired an A player, meaning the right team member for the right functional role.

HIRING AND ASSESSMENTS

Topgrading has a very specific interview process. It takes practice to learn and you have to be patient with it, but once you have the hang of it, you'll hire the right person nine times out of ten. That fact doesn't just come from my experience; it's what the creators of this methodology found as well.

I'll give you an example: In one of my companies, we were starting a new project, and we needed to hire ten new developers all at once. That seemed like a daunting task, but we had been running the Topgrading interview process for a while and we felt we were pretty good at it.

So we started the process and interviewed some candidates. We took the first candidate we liked about halfway through the process, and then we decided to hire him before we finished as we were short on time and he had the right skill set. We brought him in and soon realized we had sold ourselves short. We hadn't called references as we normally do. We hadn't asked the questions we always ask. Within a few weeks, we knew we had made a mistake.

We knew first and foremost because he didn't fit our culture. Beyond that, we soon discovered he didn't have the skills or the experience we thought he had. The Topgrading process dives deep into experience. You begin by weeding out C players (more on this in the next section) before you move to the long interview. Then, in the long interview, you ask questions that go all the way back to high school. You talk about every job the person has held up to that point.

I've done this with people who have twenty or thirty years' worth of experience, and it can take a while. But what comes out of it is really key themes about who that person is. A lot of interviewers skip the questions about high school. They are really important as a lot of your character can be traced back that far. In the last chapter, I talked about things I learned from playing on a field hockey team when I was sixteen. Talking about experiences like that helps the interviewer get at the core of who the job applicant is as a human being. And we're trying to find that out so we can see if this job applicant will fit with the team. Another important feature about this methodology is that it's really hard to hide in it.

The Topgrading process is so prescriptive that all you have to do is follow it and not waiver. If candidates don't want to invest five hours in an interview, you know they're not a good fit for your organization. You're investing all this time to get the right candidate, so wouldn't you want to know something like that up front rather than learning six months down the line that you hired the wrong person?

When we hired that new developer, we skipped a bunch of steps and we paid for it. Everyone who is hired and shouldn't have been is a huge cost to the organization. After we let the developer go, we had a quick post-mortem on how this mistake had happened. We realized that even though we had been following this process for years, we felt very stressed about having to hire ten people quickly. So, we cut corners. We didn't invest the time. Every day those positions weren't filled was hard on the rest of the team. But hiring people and training them and then realizing they're not right for the team is worse.

So, we went back and started again. We hired ten people following the process to a T. We got the first one wrong, but we got the next nine in a row right. So, we succeeded with nine out of ten, just as the methodology promises. Don't rush the process.

Once we'd hired the right team members, we used the Topgrading process to continue to assess them. We worked these assessments into our quarterly rhythm, whereby, every ninety days, we would assess our team members based on whether they were A, B, or C players. In the simplest terms, C players are people you wouldn't hire in the first place, or if they are already part of your team, you wouldn't rehire them. They do not support the company's core values.

Making this a part of your regular rhythm ensures you always have A and B players on your team. An A player is the best person you can have on your team within the range of what you can afford. That's important to understand. A lot of A players are very expensive. There are some A players who are just out of reach. B players are people who are the right fit for your team, meaning they share the company's core values but are working on improving their skills and have the potential to become A players. A C player does not fit and does not have the potential to become an A player. When we assessed people as C players, we took immediate action to remove them from our team and allow them to find a new company or team where they would fit and be successful.

PERSONAL ONE PAGE PLANS

What Topgrading provides is a solid, do-not-waiver system to bring in the best people. We started there, and then took Verne Harnish's OPP and used that to keep people on track, accountable, and focused.

Once you hire a team member, you have to be clear about what that person is accountable for. That's why, on their first day, we worked with our new team members on their own personal OPP that was clear about exactly what they were going to be measured on and accountable for in the next ninety days. Everyone in our organization had a personal OPP, which rolled all the way up to the company's OPP, which I was accountable for.

EXAMPLE OF TEAM MEMBER ONE PAGE INDIVIDUAL PLAN

Individual One Page Plan

Name: _____ Plan Type: ☐ Wk ☐ Mo ☐ Qtr ☐ Annual ☐ Other

Position: _____ Review Date: _____

Legend: 1 - Meets Expectations, 2 - Exceeds Expectations, 0 - Needs Improvement

Team top 5 and 1 of 5	My top 5 and 1 of 5—weighted value is 75%	Rating
1.	1.	
2.	2.	
3.	3.	
4.	4.	
5.	5.	

Core competencies (weighted value is 20%)		My Top 5 and 1 of 5 Average Total Rating	
1. Functional knowledge and skills— core requirements specific to job description	Rating	**Resources needed to accomplish my top 5** 1. 2. 3.	
a.			
Expectation:			
b.		**Additional Development Goals:** (weighted value is 5%)	Rating
Expectation:			
c.		1.	
Expectation:		2.	
2. Service Excellence: *(serve our customers and our teammates)* Makes serving customers and their needs a primary focus.		3.	
		Additional Development Goals Average Total Rating	
Expectation:		**Comments:**	
3. Builds and Leads a Successful Team: *(serve our customers and our teammates)* Facilitates a culture that rewards team successes.			
Expectation:			
4. Drives for Results: *(serial achievers and innovators)* Leads others to fulfill performance expectations to accomplish company goals.			
Expectation:			
5. Innovative: *(serial achievers and innovators)* Generates innovative solutions in work situations.			
Expectation:			
Core competencies average total rating			
Overall evaluation rating			

With everyone in the company holding an OPP, we then developed this process into the performance evaluation system for our team members. It fit right in with our rhythm. As I said before, on a quarterly basis we ranked our team members privately as A, B, or C players, and we did it based on how well they lived up to the values and accomplished the goals spelled out in their plans. And if we identified a C player, we did something about it.

This system made it very clear why you were joining the team, what you needed to do once you were on the team, and what the opportunities for growth were within our organization. Within your one-pager, you had the company's top goals for the next ninety days, your team's top goals for the next ninety days, and your own top goals for the next ninety days, which told you exactly how you were going to be evaluated over the next quarter. And every ninety days, every person got a new one-pager because the goals had been updated from our quarterly planning sessions.

When we first implemented this system, we had to have some hard discussions and let some people go. For example, when my first company was bought and we became part of the larger company, I was no longer the CEO. I became EVP of product and technology and acquired some new team members in the process. Some of those people weren't necessarily what I would call A or B players. In fact, they were definitely C players by my evaluation. Each addition was given a good tryout. I started out by making sure a personal OPP was created for all team members. After that, things became very obvious very quickly. C players don't like accountability. Plus, everybody's plan is wide open for everyone else in the organization to see. C players don't like that kind of transparency or the peer accountability that goes along with it. It makes it very obvious when someone is not getting results.

When someone failed to get results, our policy was that that team member would start meeting with his team leader every day for four weeks to keep him on track. When you have to get involved with someone on a daily basis, it's no fun for the leader or the team member, but it really helps the leader know whether he wants someone who needs that level of attention on his team. An A player doesn't want you in her business. The right person is someone you're going to help grow, someone you can coach on how to do things the best way possible. The wrong person, the C player, is someone you're going to have to micromanage.

I soon found out that one of the C players I had acquired on my team had been a C player in the organization for quite some time. He hadn't been successful on one team, so he'd been moved to another. He wasn't successful on that team either, so he was moved to yet another team. That's a classic C player.

What happened in this particular case is what often happens when you start the process of one-on-one daily micromanagement meetings: the team member didn't like working that way, so he put in his resignation. If the C player doesn't put in his resignation, you usually end up terminating him at the end of that period, but it often doesn't go that far. I can remember the leadership team asking me how I was getting those people to resign. Often, all you have to do is be really clear about what's expected of them and what they're accountable for, and C players will decide for themselves that it's too much to handle.

CLARITY

As the leader, you are responsible for making clear to everyone what's expected of them and how they've performed: whether they've met your expectations, exceeded your expectations, or have not met your expectations. Otherwise, they're not being held accountable for anything. That's why, when people joined our company or were team members, they each had their own OPP that rolled up to their teams' and to the overall company. There was clarity from day one on what was expected of them. And they appreciated this.

Most people are happy to have clarity, and they're unhappy when they don't have it. People who loved our interviewing process, who appreciated that we would invest that much time in making sure they were the right fit, who appreciated walking in and knowing exactly what they were accountable for on the first day, and appreciated that we evaluated their results every quarter—those are ones we wanted on our team. A person who's an A player wants that kind of clarity and is going to appreciate being rewarded for meeting or exceeding expectations. This methodology certainly helped us extract the people who didn't fit. More importantly, it helped us to focus and spend time on the A players.

I knew we really had a good system and a good rhythm going when we started the second company and everybody from the first company wanted to join. They wanted to be part of it. They wanted to have that clarity, and they understood the Metronome Effect. Right now, I don't have my own company, but I have lots of people from my first and second companies waiting to see if I'm going to build another business. It's really fun for people to be part of an organization with a known goal and an expected rhythm, one where they understand how they will fit and contribute.

GROW YOUR TEAM MEMBERS

Companies that continuously learn and foster good habits and accountability have been the most successful companies over the last hundred years. Jim Collins has spent much of his career proving this point. The human system at my companies ensured that team members grew through learning. We set a rhythm in which, written down in each person's OPP was what they were going to do to grow themselves professionally that quarter. This could be reading a book on a specific skill area related to their functional role or attending a workshop or conference. The key was that we made this a part of our human system. It was one of our core values and we were prepared to plan and invest in these learning opportunities regularly in our rhythm, both personally and corporately. A players want to learn and grow, and by working this into your human system, you will keep your A players.

DRIVING PERFORMANCE

Your last step for ensuring you have an effective human system is to get a personal OPP into the hands of everyone across the organization. I believe it's fundamental to any business of any size for everybody to have an OPP that ties into the performance-review process. Most people think this is a daunting task, and I don't disagree, but it's so achievable if you take it step by step.

You won't pull it off in one quarter. In fact, it will take a minimum of eight quarters to make it happen. That scares a lot of people, but I remind them that in eight quarters it's going to be an ingrained, habitual beat within your organization that causes all your players to show up, knowing exactly what's going to happen. They're going to understand how to contribute within the beat that you set.

A lot of people thought we were crazy to extend this system to all 200-plus people in our company, but laying it all out there, writing it down, and then following up every ninety days with an evaluation made it certain we would execute our plan.

The Metronome Effect methodology ensured that we were checking all boxes and taking all the right steps each and every day, week, month, quarter, and year. I end on the human system because it was the final piece that ensured I had all the right team members in the right roles with the right skills, growing and loving it continuously!

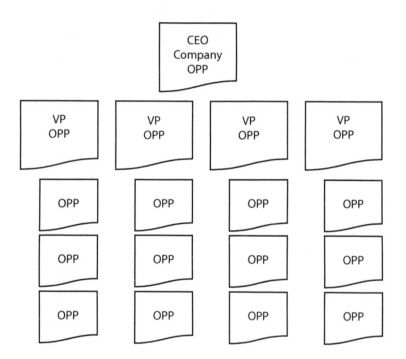

The hierarchy of the OPPs above is perfection. It took us over eight quarters to reach all 200-plus team members with an OPP that was tied tightly to our human system and cohesive team, strategy, and execution plans. This is the picture of the journey the Metronome Effect methodology takes you on to reach predictable profit.

SETTING THE BEAT

Once the OPP is being used by all direct reports for at least three quarters, work with your leadership team to create an OPP for all team members.

ACTION ITEMS

1. Read the book *Topgrading* by Brad Smart, or *Who: The A Method for Hiring* by Geoff Smart, or attend a Topgrading workshop.

2. Use the Topgrading system for hiring and assessing talent to ensure you have all A and B players on your team.

3. When you have the OPP working in your organization for more than four quarters and all your direct reports have their own OPP, start working team by team to create an OPP for all team members. Download the Individual One Page Plan Template at www.metronome-effect.com

4. Once all members of the team have an OPP, use this in your regular 90 day review process of each team member.

CHAPTER 12

THE METRONOME EFFECT: TRUST IS EXECUTION

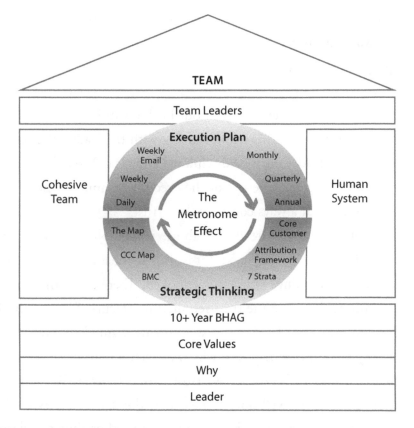

When each one of my organizations was acquired, I had at least a two-year contract to work within the acquiring firm. That meant I had to go into a totally new culture, one that I didn't create with my team. With my first company, rightly or wrongly, I kept my team pretty much intact and mostly out of the larger culture for a while. We were remote, far away from the head office, and I was pretty much the only executive who ever went to that office, so it was fairly easy to stay aligned and keep our culture intact.

But as time went on, we had to integrate. During that period, we were involved with other teams and we definitely had some problems. My team could easily see that across the entire company there wasn't the same belief in what the company was doing, there wasn't the same drive for results, and there weren't the same behaviours that lead to results. That was a really trying time for us.

It wasn't until my second company was bought and I had spent a couple years in the larger acquiring organization that it really became clear to me that a culture of trust was the way to get things done. So, I sat down with the leaders of our business unit and took them through everything in this book, starting with the leader. We talked about how the leader must be disciplined and clear. We talked about how he owns the cohesiveness of the executive team, and how that starts with trust. It always comes back to trust.

Many people will read the above paragraph and think it's obvious. It sounds so simple, and it is. But at the end of the day, it's often the simple things that get overlooked. There aren't that many organizations that have the trust required to execute. When I think about why the team from my first company wanted to work with me in my second company and why they would join me in my next company, I know it's because we trusted one another. Beyond my own experience, it's well documented that the companies with the best cultures, the ones that have been recognized as the best places to work, are also the ones that outperformed other companies in the down market of 2008.

As a leader, if you build trust first, you can have that cohesive team. By having a consistent human system in place, by being self-aware and taking real action on a timely basis, and by over-communicating so you have clarity, you can stay cohesive.

From there, a leader needs to work with the leadership team to develop that ten-year BHAG, and three-year targets based on the strategy created. In order to achieve that, there has to be belief, ownership, and empowerment. Trusting and believing go hand in hand, and in order for people to believe, you've got to have a strong business model. You've got to know how to go to market. You've got to know your value proposition and your position in the marketplace. There has to be belief in all these things from every member of the leadership team. And the way you get that belief is for the leadership team to create these things together.

I talked earlier about how, during the bubble years, my company hired a lot of people who shared our core values and fit our culture. They didn't all have the exact skill set we wanted, but we knew we could get them there and that, because they fit well, they would stay with us a long time. Some of the people who started out this way grew to become members of our executive team and came with me from my first company to my second. It was an incredible journey with them, and I think all leaders want to have that kind of relationship with their team.

THE METRONOME EFFECT CAN SET YOU FREE

This book means to challenge you and your leadership team to put a metronomic rhythm in place that will help you achieve the results you want. The rhythm must regularly incorporate core ideologies, team cohesiveness, the human system, as well as your strategic analysis and execution plan. One of the most important aspects of setting the metronome is that it creates a culture that makes people want to show up to work with each other every day. It also makes them want to stick with you, even through difficult times. They know what's going to happen every day, they know what's expected of them, they can see where they're going, and they can celebrate the results. That kind of clarity creates trust and accountability.

If you've done all the work up to this point and you've done it well, then you're likely to be in a place where you have a trusted team and trusted processes. And that trust means you can count on the metronome to keep beating. Even when you walk away, the metronome will keep beating.

The beat you set with your metronome becomes an expected habit within your organization that can really free up the leader's time. That's something I needed when I first discovered Verne Harnish. But adding the discipline of team cohesiveness, the human system and the foundational values to a solid execution rhythm freed up my time to think about the business, to ensure we were driving towards the right things, both operationally and strategically, and to ensure my people were taken care of. But it also freed up my time so I could have balance in my life. I went from working seven days a week to working a regular workweek. I had just gotten married, and then I had three kids in less than three years. It was mayhem. I'm very thankful for the Metronome Effect methodology because of how it improved both my personal and professional life. There was no more getting caught in the weeds every day.

I used to travel a great deal in both my businesses, but I felt confident doing so because I knew the beat would always be there, regardless of whether or not I could show up for every meeting. If I was on a plane or overseas, I'd do my best to call in to our regular meetings, but sometimes I couldn't. It didn't matter. The beat went on.

It will take some time, so don't be discouraged if the beat doesn't become a habit within the first quarter. It can take up to eight quarters to get a solid metronome beat going across the organization. It will likely take two or three quarters to get it in place with your management team. Because it can take time, I encourage you set up the expectation right away. I always recommend doing this by starting a daily huddle.

Once you get the rhythm in place, you can use this book to brush up on any part of the methodology where you might be falling behind. If you find your team faltering in a particular area, go back to the chapter on team cohesiveness and reread it. This book doesn't have to be read from beginning to end.

I read certain books every year, including those by thought leaders whose wisdom I have pulled together to form this methodology. Every year I either read or listen to (because I'm in the car a lot) *Good to Great* by Jim Collins, *Built to Last* by Jim Collins and Jerry Porras, and *The Five Dysfunctions of a Team* and *The Five Temptations of a CEO* by Patrick Lencioni. I get something different out of them every year because every year I'm dealing with different situations, different people, and different challenges. I hope it will be the same for you with this book. You can go back to any chapter at any time to help you address a particular challenge, but I also encourage you to read the book through every year, or at least read the Action Items at the end of each chapter, to make sure you aren't missing any foundational items.

Once you get your metronome rhythm in place and you've worked through these tools, you should always be looking at these tools or for new tools. This methodology will become habit, something you can count on year after year to ensure you're growing, your profit is predictable, and you're getting the results you want.

The last thing I would say to leaders—and this comes from my own leadership style—is to remember to lead by example. Be very clear in your behavior. Make your intent known. Make sure your assumptions always lean towards the positive, not the negative, and that your behavior is an example for others to follow.

That comes from reflecting on seventeen years of doing this, of having the opportunity to build teams within my own organizations and then take those teams into other organizations and keep them intact while also integrating into a new culture. It comes from working as a coach or consultant with hundreds of business leaders from other organizations. It has been a very interesting journey for sure.

This is a journey to predictable profit and you must be patient and take baby steps. Set your metronome today.

APPENDIX: SUGGESTED READING LIST

ARTICLES

"The Five Competitive Forces that Shape Strategy" by Michael E Porter, *Harvard Business Review*, January 2008.

"What is Strategy" by Michael E Porter, *Harvard Business Review*, November 1996.

"Building Your Company's Vision" by James C. Collins and Jerry I. Porras, *Harvard Business Review*, September 1996.

BOOKS

Behind The Cloud by Mark Benioff and Carlyle Adler

Built to Last by Jim Collins and Jerry Porras

The Business Model Generation by Alexander Osterwalder

Competitive Strategy by Michael E Porter

Crossing the Chasm by Geoffrey Moore

Delivering Happiness by Tony Hsieh

Double Double by Cameron Herold

The Five Temptations of a CEO by Patrick Lencioni

The Five Dysfunctions of a Team by Patrick Lencioni

The Four Obsessions of an Extraordinary Executive by Patrick Lencioni

Good to Great by Jim Collins

Mastering the Rockefeller Habits by Verne Harnish

Scaling Up: How to Build a Meaningful Business ... and Enjoy the Ride by Verne Harnish

Speed of Trust by Stephen Covey

Strengths Finder 2.0 by Tom Rath

Topgrading: How to Hire, Coach, and Keep A Players by Brad Smart

appendix: Setting the Metronome

JOURNEY TO PREDICTABLE PROFIT CHECKLIST

Chapter	What	Who	Frequency
1	Know your personal 'why'.	CEO	Quarterly
1	Read Patrick Lencioni's *The Five Temptations of a CEO*. Write down your biggest temptation and share them with team members.	CEO	Annually
1	*Strengths Finder 2.0 Assessment* by Tom Rath	CEO and whole team overtime.	Quarterly
1	Cameron Herold's Painted Picture	CEO	Quarterly
1	Book professional development in your calendar for 12 months	CEO	Annually
2	Functional Accountability Chart (FACe)	CEO Leadership Team	Quarterly
2	Ask yourself, 'Would I enthusiastically rehire everyone on my team?' If the answer is no, this must be addressed.	CEO Leadership Team	Quarterly
2	Create an environment map—The Map	CEO Leadership Team	Quarterly
2	Verne Harnish's Cash Acceleration Strategies (CASh) Worksheet	CEO Leadership Team	Quarterly
2	Cash Conversion Flow Chart	CEO Leadership Team	Quarterly

3	Establish a core purpose for the company. Make the company's core purpose known throughout the organization.	CEO Leadership Team	Quarterly
3	Establish core values by utilizing Jim Collins' Mars Exercise. Make these values known to the team. Integrate them into your human system.	CEO Leadership Team	Quarterly
3	Even if you're unsure, 'gut it out' and write down a Big Hairy Audacious Goal.	CEO Leadership Team	Quarterly
3	Live by your core purpose, core values, and BHAG and make them an integral part of your organization. They should be a key part of your hiring and performance review processes and they should be talked about often. Over-communicate the message!	CEO Leadership Team	Quarterly
4	Review Michael Porter's Five Forces framework, as a team, and fill out his Analysis Worksheet to see where the power lies in your industry.	CEO Leadership Team	Quarterly
4	Review Porter's Five Forces analysis, as a team, and compare or overlay it to on your Map.	CEO Leadership Team	Quarterly
4	Create an Activity Map that shows what activities differentiate you from your competitors.	CEO Leadership Team	Quarterly
5	Geoffrey Moore's Positioning Statement Template	CEO Leadership Team	Quarterly
5	Geoffrey Moore's Value Proposition Template	CEO Leadership Team	Quarterly
5	Alexander Osterwadler Business Model Canvas	CEO Leadership Team	Quarterly
6	Core customer—by completing the 6 Steps outlined in Chapter 6 based on Bob Bloom's book *Inside Advantage*.	CEO Leadership Team	Quarterly

6	Create with your team an Attribution framework for your company and specific segments if this applies.	CEO Leadership Team	Quarterly
6	Verne Harnish, Seven Strata framework with your team.	CEO Leadership Team	Quarterly
7	Verne Harnish's OPP	CEO Leadership Team	Quarterly
8	Plan your annual slate of meetings and communication.	CEO	Annually
8	Create and make known your standing agendas for all meetings and communication.	CEO	Quarterly
8	Book and start your daily huddles this week.	CEO	Daily
8	Support your leadership team with their team meetings to prepare for the leadership meetings.	CEO	Quarterly
9	Revisit your Cash Conversion Flow Chart	CEO Leadership Team	Quarterly Review
9	Forecast profit: Create a thirty-six-month, month-over-month financial forecast.	CEO Leadership Team	Annually Quarterly Review
9	Line up your OPP with your financial forecast.	CEO Leadership Team	Annually Quarterly Review
10	Read the *Five Dysfunctions of a Team* by Patrick Lencioni or attend a facilitated workshop to jump-start your understanding.	CEO Leadership Team	Annually
10	Use Lencioni's online tools or facilitator's guide to assess your team's cohesiveness in each of the five areas.	CEO Leadership Team	Annually or as often as required
10	Work through all Five Dysfunctions with your team on a continual basis to stay on track.	CEO Leadership Team	Quarterly
11	Read the book *Topgrading* by Brad Smart or *Who: The A Method for Hiring* by Geoff Smart or attend a Topgrading workshop.	CEO Leadership Team	As soon as possible

11	Use the Topgrading system for hiring and assessing talent to ensure you have all A and B players on your team.	CEO Leadership Team	Immediately
11	When you have the OPP working in your organization for more than four quarters and all your direct reports have their own OPP, start working team by team to create an OPP for all team members.	CEO Leadership Team	After four quarters of OPP at the leadership team level
11	Once all members of the team have an OPP, use this in your regular review process of each team member.	Leadership Team	Quarterly

WWW.METRONOME-EFFECT.COM

CPSIA information can be obtained
at www.ICGtesting.com
Printed in the USA
FFHW011839291019
55844502-61722FF